The Police
of Britain

The Police
of Britain

Philip John Stead

MACMILLAN PUBLISHING COMPANY
A Division of Macmillan, Inc.
NEW YORK

Collier Macmillan Publishers
LONDON

Macmillan Publishing Company
A Division of Macmillan, Inc.
866 Third Avenue, New York, N. Y. 10022

Collier Macmillan Canada, Inc.

Library of Congress Catalog Card Number: 84–17184

Printed in the United States of America

printing number
1   2   3   4   5   6   7   8   9   10

Library of Congress Cataloging in Publication Data

Stead, Philip John.
    The police of Britain.

    Bibliography: p.
    Includes index.
    1. Police—Great Britain—History.   I. Title.
HV8195.A2S725   1985   363.2′0941   84–17184
ISBN 0-02-930760-0

For

Ian A. Watt
M.A. (Aberdeen), M.A. (Oxon)
Dean of Academic Studies
The Police Staff College, Bramshill

this small token of a great regard

Contents

Preface

This survey of the history and organization of the British police, like its predecessor, *The Police of France,* published in 1983, arose from lectures and seminars given at the Police Staff College, Bramshill, England; John Jay College of Criminal Justice, City University of New York; and the Ecole Nationale Supérieure de Police, France. It therefore owes much in matter and presentation to the questions and interests of my students, many of whom now hold high rank in the police services of the three countries.

I have given most space to the police systems of England and Wales, but I have included information about the other police systems within the United Kingdom of Great Britain and Northern Ireland, and British policing overseas.

The Police of France and *The Police of Britain* both are designed to serve as basic texts for the historical and comparative study of police, the one describing the police system most eminently illustrative of the Roman Law tradition, the other of the Common Law tradition shared by Britain, the United States, and the British Commonwealth of Nations.

P.J.S.

Acknowledgments

Anyone attempting a survey of British police development must be indebted, as I am, to those who already have explored and mapped the subject, especially to Melville Lee and Charles Reith, Sir Leon Radzinowicz and Mr. T.A. Critchley.

I am particularly grateful to Mr. K.A.L. Parker, C.B., under whom I had the pleasure of serving in my Home Office days, for reading and commenting most helpfully on the manuscript of the book. His great experience as a police administrator at the Home Office and as Receiver for the Metropolitan Police District was generously made available to me.

I also wish to thank for their help Sir John Hermon, O.B.E., Chief Constable of the Royal Ulster Constabulary; Sir Philip Knights, C.B.E., Q.P.M., Chief Constable of the West Midlands Police; Mr Ian T. Oliver, LL.B., M.Phil., Chief Constable of the Central Scotland Police; Mr. Robert P. Bryan, O.B.E., Overseas Police Adviser and Inspector-General of Police, Dependent Territories at the Foreign and Commonwealth Office; Mr. David Powis, O.B.E., Q.P.M., Deputy Assistant Commissioner in charge of Operations, Criminal Investigation Department, New Scotland

Yard; Mr. C.G.A.Parker, J.P., M.A.; Professor John J. Cronin, Department of Law, Police Science and Criminal Justice Administration, and Professor Eileen Rowland, Chief Librarian, John Jay College of Criminal Justice, City University of New York.

Thanks are due to the following publishers for their permission to quote passages acknowledged in the text:

Messrs. A. and C. Black Ltd (Sir Percival Griffiths's *To Guard My People*); Messrs. McGraw-Hill Book Company (U.K.) Ltd (David Powis's *The Signs of Crime*); Messrs. Patterson Smith (*Pioneers in Policing*); and Messrs. Sweet and Maxwell Ltd (Henry Cecil's *The English Judge*). Messrs. R. Hazell Ltd kindly gave permission for maps to be reproduced from their publication *The Police and Constabulary Almanac*.

The Police
of Britain

CHAPTER 1

Government and Police
in Britain

The Governmental Structure

The United Kingdom of Great Britain and Northern Ireland comprises England and Wales, Scotland, and Northern Ireland. Its constitution, unlike those of most modern democracies, is not contained in a single document. It is to be found in the statutes and decided cases of the Common Law, and in conventions—rules that do not have the force of law and resemble the unwritten rules that enable families and other social organisms to function effectively. Ancillary, but influential, the works of political philosophers and other writers also have their place in the miscellaneous scheme of the British constitution.

Anyone accustomed to rigid adherence to the doctrine of separation of powers must find Britain's constitutional model anomalous. A monarchy—in a democracy? An executive—in the legislature? A judicial system in which the legislature is the highest court? The monarchy, however, takes only a ceremonial part in the governmental process: its principal function is symbolic, incarnating the headship not only of the United Kingdom but also the

British Commonwealth of Nations. The supreme power is located in Parliament.

There are two houses of Parliament. The House of Lords, "Lords Spiritual and Temporal," the senior chamber, is not elective. Those entitled to sit and vote there are twenty-six bishops of the Church of England, nearly one thousand hereditary peers, ten judges, and some three hundred peers and peeresses appointed for life by reason of their eminence in service to the nation. Such a large assembly, were it to meet in its entirety, would be unwieldy in the extreme, but the usual attendance is under three hundred. The legislative power of the Lords has been severely curtailed over the years and is puny indeed compared with that of the United States Senate; the Lords can, in some instances, delay but never veto bills from the lower house.

In the House of Commons sit 635 elected members of Parliament. These are the dominant partners in the trinity: Queen, Lords, Commons—a trinity expressed in the formula, "The Queen (or the King) in Parliament." It is the majority party in the Commons that provides the ministers of the executive government and initiates the chief legislation. Thus, despite the nonelective elements of monarch and peers, the supreme power is in the hands of those returned to Parliament by the national electorate.

The supremacy of the British Parliament may be measured by the fact that no court of justice in the land has the power to invalidate its acts. The United States Supreme Court of Justice, in its constitutional jurisdiction, has absolutely no parallel in Britain.

The day-to-day business of government demands comprehensive, administrative machinery. The political ministers responsible for the departments of state, e.g., the Treasury, the Ministry of Defense, the Foreign and Commonwealth Office, the Department of Health and Social Security, and the Home Office, are each served by a bureaucracy staffed by the national civil service. The bureaucratic hierarchy rises to the level immediately below the political ministers, the senior civil servant being known as the Permanent Under-Secretary of State. For the actions of their officials, the ministers are answerable to Parliament.

The differences between this system and that of the United States are radical. First, the heads of the executive government, the ministers, all sit in Parliament, either in the Commons or the

Lords (it is now a well-established convention that the prime minister be a member of the lower house), as opposed to the constitutional rule in the United States that members of the executive government (save the vice president) cannot sit in the legislature. Second, the permanent civil service in Britain assures administrative continuity and has administrative influence far exceeding its more fluid counterpart in the United States, where a change of government means a change of the higher echelons of the federal bureaucracy. The British term "civil servant," incidentally, refers only to the officials of the national government; local governments have their hierarchies of officials, too, but these are called "local government officers."

Traditionally strong and jealous of its turf, local government in Britain has undergone great changes during the last quarter of a century, the main result of which has been a two-thirds reduction in the number of local authorities.

In England and Wales there are now 47 counties, each of which has a county council. Each county area contains districts or boroughs (333 in all), which also have councils. The councils at county, district, and borough level are independent of one another and have distinct functions. The county council, for instance, deals with major planning affecting the whole area, the highways (main roads), education, refuse disposal, fire, and police. The district or borough council deals with local planning, housing, public hygiene, refuse collection, and passenger transport.

There are, at the time of this writing, six "super counties," called metropolitan counties, grouping in all thirty-five metropolitan districts or metropolitan boroughs, but it is expected that the metropolitan counties will be abolished in the course of the next year or two. Some of their functions, including police, will be assigned to ad hoc bodies.

London and its suburbs, Greater London, is not one of the six metropolitan counties just mentioned. The Greater London Council operates in the overall area, within which there are thirty-two boroughs.

At the lowest level of local government there are parish councils, parish meetings, and town councils, with functions commensurate with the size and nature of the community and area.

All local authorities are elective.

Local government in Britain, independent as it is in many respects, does not enjoy anything like the independence of local government in the United States, where the states of the Union have legislative, executive and judicial powers unknown to any local British authority. The two systems of local government reflect the profound differences between a "unitary" and a "federal" constitution.

Britain's central government has a far stronger hand in its dealings with local government than has the federal government in the United States. The contribution from national taxes to local services is massive, and the central government has taken measures to ensure that its money is properly spent, e.g., by audit, inspection, or inquiry. Ministerial approval of certain actions by local authorities is required. Parliament has legislated widely in the local government sphere (all local government authorities exist in virtue of Acts of Parliament), and the need to observe the laws exercises continual control.

The interaction of central and local government is particularly evident in the control of the police.

The Control of the Police

The ministry of the central government principally concerned with law and order in England and Wales has as its political head Her Majesty's Secretary of State for the Home Department—the home secretary. Among this minister's responsibilities, which include the administration of justice and the criminal law, extradition, immigration and aliens, the prison, probation and aftercare services, and the fire service, one of the most important is the responsibility for the police.

This responsibility is of different kinds. First, the home secretary is directly responsible for the largest of Britain's police forces, the Metropolitan Police of London, and answerable to Parliament for his control of it. In practice this means that the sphere of overall policy for the force is his, while operational control and detailed administration rest with the commissioner of the force.

Over the other forty-two police forces in England and Wales, the minister's control is only partial; it is shared with the local authorities of the area concerned. The local police authority, two-thirds of the membership being from the elected council of the area and one-third from the local justices of the peace, is responsible under statute for securing the maintenance of an adequate and efficient police force for its area.

The home secretary's statutory duty is to promote the efficiency of the police in general. This duty he discharges in various ways. He is empowered to pay half the cost of a local police force from national taxes, the other half coming from locally imposed taxes, provided that he is satisfied that the force is efficient. This he ascertains by having each force regularly inspected by senior officials of his department: Her Majesty's Inspectors of Constabulary. It is only after one of the inspectors has certified the force efficient that the national contribution can be paid to the local authority. It is a powerful control mechanism, and the national grant has not had to be withheld within living memory; the existence of the power to withhold has in practice proved sufficient.

In many matters it is necessary for the home secretary to give his approval of steps by the police authority. Though the latter appoints the chief, deputy, and assistant chiefs of police, the appointments must have the minister's approval, as must any request by the authority for the chief officer to resign. Local police expenditure is subject to the minister's approval, though in practice there is a great deal of devolution. The minister also is empowered to make regulations for the administration and conditions of service of the force.

The partnership, therefore, of the local authority and the minister is both financial (the total police expenditure for England and Wales in 1982 was over two billion pounds sterling—about three billion dollars) and administrative. To this partnership must be admitted a third active member, the chief officer of police, commander of the force. To him is reserved the direction and control of the force: recruitment, training, promotion up to and including the rank of chief superintendent, discipline, deployment, and operations. His autonomy in these respects is, nevertheless, subject to the financial control of the local authority and the requirement to report annually to the authority, and the home secretary, on the policing of the area. It is also subject to the minister's power to call for special reports or institute local inquiries.

This triple partnership must seem strange to Americans, involving as it does such powerful intervention by the British equivalent of the federal government in the business of local police administration. It is an outstanding example of the English capacity for compromise, a formula in which both national and local politicians exercise a measure of control, while the professionals enjoy virtual independence in their maintenance of the peace and enforcement of the law. Needless to say, police authorities and chief officers do not always agree as to the precise dividing line between their respective responsibilities, but generally it has been possible to reach a *modus vivendi*.

How all this has come about is the subject of the following chapters.

CHAPTER 2

The Old Order

Beginnings

An unarmed officer, helmeted, in a dark blue uniform, against the background of a street: such is the image usually evoked of the British police.

That figure has been traced to its remote origins in the tribal customs of the Germanic peoples who invaded and settled in Britain during the period from the fifth to the seventh century A.D., but our first organized police system antedates the Teutonic conquest.

Britain, northernmost part of the Roman Empire, was administered in much the same way as other Roman provinces, with civil and military officers enforcing the law. The police element was provided largely by the army, soldiers being detached from the legions for police duties: maintaining order, apprehending wrongdoers, bringing them before the judges. The communal life of Britain, during most of the Roman occupation, was tranquil, and there were fine cities in the grand Roman style.

When the legions were withdrawn in the earlier part of the

fifth century, the romanized Britons proved no match for the invaders from northern Europe (Angles, Saxons, and Jutes, according to Beda, writing in the eighth century). The Teutonic conquest of the country that now bears their name—the "Land of the Angles," England—was so complete that apart from some place names, only three or four words of the Celtic language of Britain survive in English today. In Wales and Scotland the older inhabitants of the island retained their individuality and their language.

The coming of the Germanic barbarians, in Britain as elsewhere, swept away all the administrative machinery of Rome: the cities were deserted; all centralization was lost in the welter of tribalism, until kingship evolved and eventually a monarch ruled England. Under these circumstances, where tribal localism took vigorous root, the English police system emerged.

The territorial divisions of the Anglo-Saxon kingdom were the "shires," also called counties after the Norman Conquest, which were subdivided into "hundreds" (i.e., the area inhabited by one hundred families) and the hundreds were divided into "tithings," the neighborhood of some ten or a dozen families. To these families, in the persons of the householders, devolved the responsibility for peace keeping and law enforcement. Each year one of the householders acted as the tithing's representative and answered for his neighbors to the "hundredman," the householder representing all the tithings of the hundred, and he in turn had to answer to the "reeve" of the shire, sometimes called the "royal reeve" because he was appointed by the king, in whom may be seen the sheriff of later times. Such was the basic police system of Saxon England, constituted on the principle of collective responsibility, the community binding itself to keep the peace and deliver anyone who broke it to the courts of the hundred or the shire.

It would be oversimplifying the matter to imply that all Anglo-Saxon policing could be reduced to this model, for it must be recognized that many powerful people, such as nobles and churchmen, exercised their own jurisdiction and held their own courts.

This amalgam of police organizations continued after the Norman Conquest, when the shire-hundred-tithing system offered an effective method of control, exercised on the king's behalf by the Norman sheriff. In the twelfth century we find the tithing's police responsibility being referred to in documents as "frankpledge"

(English for the Latin *plegium liberale,* i.e., "the pledge of a free man"), and though the frankpledge system was never universally adopted in Norman England, it has great historical significance.

Frankpledge perpetuated the Anglo-Saxon principle of local police responsibility, embodying the ancient concept of "suretyship," with the householders of the tithing entering into joint responsibility for any crime committed by anyone in the tithing and for bringing the offender to justice: in default, all must pay. As its English historian W.A. Morris has written, frankpledge "was a system of compulsory, collective bail, fixed for individuals not after their arrest for crime but as a safeguard in anticipation of it." In old English law, though not in fact (for in several shires there was no frankpledge and local strong men were independent of it), every free man was required to be a member of a tithing.

The successful operation of the system depended on its being overseen by royal officials—sheriffs making their rounds of the localities, inquiring into the state of crime, enforcing the attendance of the representatives of the hundreds and the tithings, and taking action on their presentations—but the legacy of frankpledge is that the local community be responsible for law and order, as opposed to the Roman idea of paid officials of the imperial government assuming this duty. The first English policemen, then, were ordinary citizens, taking their turn of unpaid duty.

During the Middle Ages, the life of cities was regenerated, and as in so many countries, urban needs required new police initiatives. The principal piece of legislation in this respect dates from the reign of Edward I and the Statute of Winchester of 1285. Its preamble quaintly foreshadows our modern predicament:

> Forasmuch as from Day to Day, Robberies, Murthers, Burnings, and Theft, be more often used than they have been heretofore, and Felons cannot be attainted by the Oath of Jurors, which had rather suffer Strangers to be robbed and so pass without Pain, than to indite the Offenders.

The statute only repeats older laws in its emphasis on the local community's responsibility for law enforcement, but it broke newer ground in requiring that the gates of walled towns be closed from sunset to sunrise, and that the inhabitants provide a night watch to arrest strangers and bring them before the sheriff, though again the statute is reaffirming earlier law and custom. A royal writ of 1253 had ordered "That watches be held in the several townships as hath been wont, and by honest and able men."

The act stresses the ancient responsibility of raising the hue and cry to pursue and apprehend criminals, and also repeats the requirement that every man between the ages of fifteen and sixty possess arms according to his station in life. Inspections were ordered to be made to ensure that those concerned were actually in possession of the arms prescribed, and it is in this connection that one comes across the word "constables" as the name of those who were to carry out the inspection. Who these constables were appears from the royal writ of 1253, which requires that "two free and lawful men be chosen from the most powerful in each hundred" to supervise the enforcement of the law. It is easy to believe that these "high constables," as they were later called, assumed the old responsibilities of the hundredmen.

About this time it seems that the word constable also was used to denote the tithingman, in this case referred to as the "petty constable," as distinct from the high constable of the hundred. This justifies Patrick Colquhoun's magisterial pronouncement that "the office of constable is as old as the monarchy of England." During this period, the territorial unit of the tithing was replaced by the parish as the basic unit of local administration, and the petty constable generally was known as the parish constable, though both terms continued to be used interchangeably for centuries.

The parish constable, direct ancestor of the police constable of today, must be seen in a dual capacity: on one hand, he represents his fellow citizens; on the other, he represents the law of the land. From the outset, first as tithingman, then as constable, he is a private person with public duties, never an official of the central government.

The sheriff had very great power under the first Norman kings, but his rapacity led him to abuse it. This moved the monarchy to create other offices whereby that of the sheriff could be lessened. One of these was that of the coroner, chosen at the county level since the year 1194, when he was given the function, that coroners still perform, of inquiring into any unexplained death, as well as inquiring into housebreakings and other suspicious matters. This encroached markedly on the criminal jurisdiction of the sheriff.

Another new office was that of the justice of the peace, recognizable in its modern form as early as 1361, when an act of Edward III prescribed:

> In every county in England there shall be assigned for the keeping of the peace, one lord, and with him three or four of the most worthy men in the county, together with some learned in the law, and they shall have power to restrain offenders, rioters, and other barretors, and to pursue, arrest, take and chastise them, according to their trespass or offence; and to cause them to be arrested and duly punished according to the law and custom of the realm.

Here again was a great encroachment on the sheriff's criminal business.

Thus, over six hundred years ago and more there appeared in England officers of the law, constables, coroners, justices of the peace, sheriffs, who still function in Britain and whose counterparts have functioned, since colonial times, in America.

Their vitality is amply demonstrated by the fact of their survival amid the upheavals of the centuries after the Norman Conquest. Great and prolonged wars were fought; plague de-populated town and countryside; peasants rose in revolt; kings were assassinated and killed in battle; nobles destroyed one another in internecine war; a shattering religious revolution was forced through; a king fought Parliament and died on the scaffold; during a republican interlude, a military police was briefly superimposed on the old police system. Yet the restoration of the monarchy in 1660 found county justices and parish constables as fixed a feature of the country's administration as they had been in the Middle Ages.

Decline

The courts of the justices of the peace gradually took over the criminal jurisdiction of the sheriffs, and the business of the manorial courts dwindled as the scope of the magistrates' courts increased. Some offenses became triable by a justice sitting alone or with a colleague. Four times a year the justices of the county held their quarter sessions, when they sat in judgment of the more serious criminal cases, unless these presented legal difficulties, in which case they were referred to the professional judges of the king's courts. At these sessions they also acted as administrators of the county's affairs, a major local government function that they continued to perform until late in the nineteenth century.

The control of crime and disorder was largely a matter for the local justice of the peace. To him the constable brought offenders; from him he received warrants and orders. Justice and constable were both unpaid; the justice held court in his own home; the constable, once his duties were done, returned to his daily work.

This worked well enough in a predominantly agricultural and static society, but as the Middle Ages drew to an end the increase of urban populations as well as the movement caused by the volume of trade and the scarcity of labor strained local peace keeping and law enforcement. The amount of crime in the cities and on the roads became an intolerable burden on an expressly nonprofessional infrastructure of justice and police.

Justices and constables alike sought relief. The country justices, landowners holding court on their estates among their tenants, were least affected. Their urban counterparts became increasingly reluctant to accept an ever busier office that involved the daily arrival at their houses of the unsavory offenders whom the constables and the watchmen had apprehended during the night. Substantial men declined to become justices and their places were taken by persons much less respectable, whose sole object was to make as much as they could out of the business of the court. Those of the stamp of Shakespeare's justice,

> In fair round belly with good capon lined,
> With eyes severe and beard of formal cut,
> Full of wise saws and modern instances,

left the magisterial bench to "trading justices," most of whom in London held court in their shops and, like Fielding's Justice Thrasher in *Amelia* (1751), were never impartial unless they could get nothing on either side of the cause.

The parish constables could not refuse to serve their year of office when appointed to it. The office, though, could be served by a deputy, by paying someone else to perform its duties. The deputy constable became a familiar figure in law enforcement, often being singularly ill suited to the task. Shakespeare, in *Measure for Measure* (1604–05), introduces such a character in Elbow, who has deputized for no less than eight appointees: "I do it for some piece of money, and go through with all." The practice was only too convenient; middle-class men and skilled laborers could not afford to neglect their livelihood for the constables' time-consuming, unremunerative, and often hazardous business. Patrick Colquhoun, in 1803, stated that in London there were 330 deputy constables, paid by the persons for whom they were substituting; John Wade, in 1829, just at the end of the old era, said that the constables "generally" employed deputies.

The Statute of Winchester had required that cities were to provide a night watch. Originally performed by the householders, the duties of the watch soon proved too troublesome for the good citizens. Paid watchmen took their place, employed at first by those nominated for the duty, later by the parish, poor service reflecting poor remuneration. At the end of the sixteenth century, Shakespeare could depict the watchmen as a comic and lamentable crew, and in the middle of the eighteenth century Fielding dismissed them as feeble and useless.

Expedients

During the late seventeenth century, after the dislocations of the Civil War, the Commonwealth, and the restoration of the monarchy in 1660, the insufficiency of the medieval police machinery became painfully apparent. As Melville Lee, first historian of the English police, wrote, "Crime follows impunity." Not only was the time-honored system structurally inadequate for the needs of a more populous and more mobile society, it was also impaired by the corruption of trading justices, deputy constables, and ill-paid watchmen, which brought discredit upon those who honestly and perseveringly discharged their duties.

The problem was worst in London. Paradoxically, and as it so often has been and is today in many countries, the seat of the legislature, the executive government and the judiciary was preeminent for its crime and disorder.

Perhaps more was stolen in London because in London there was more to steal, and indeed vast and ostentatious wealth may well be provocative of crime, but the problem had many elements.

In the capital of Augustan England, as in Augustan Rome, over-building had resulted in mazes of crazy tenements, overcrowded from cellar to garret, festering against tall streets of graceful townhouses and spacious mansions. A world of destitution coexisted with a world of opulence; a world of idleness, incapacity and deprivation coexisted with a world of work and leisure. The lower levels of society were being corroded by alcoholism, cheap spirits being universally available, delusory panacea for hunger and misery, as depicted in William Hogarth's great and terrible picture, "Gin Lane." Prostitution of children and adults was rife. Ill-lighted and unlighted streets at night, whose dirtiness was a byword in the daylight, bad drainage, and unregulated traffic, all contributed to a confusion which was accepted as a normal hazard of London life.

Crime in eighteenth-century London was more formidable than at any time in the capital's history. Constantly recruited from the greedy work shy and the starving unemployed, the criminal element's main field of recruitment was the youngsters who had run wild in the slums since infancy. These were especially active as pickpockets and sneak-thieves, with which the streets and shops, theaters and all places of public resort were plagued.

During crime waves it is common for criminals to be lionized, possibly because most people have a secret longing to rise above the law and so find gratification in the example of someone who has done so either spectacularly or with long immunity. Highwaymen often enjoyed this kind of perverse adulation, notably when impudent bravado led them to rob the Lord Mayor of London in the suburbs, and the prime minister in Piccadilly; the writers succeeded in turning even such a squalid ruffian as Richard Turpin into a popular hero. Jack Sheppard, another highway robber, at least earned his notoriety by several skillful and daring escapes from custody.

The fear of housebreaking is reflected in the design of eighteenth-century houses, whose gracious style encompassed barred windows, stout doors, and heavy shutters. To venture forth after dark was risky unless one was preceded by linkbearers and escorted by armed servants. Security measures flourished, as always, in proportion to the fear of crime, a fear which the constables and the watch did little to allay.

The hectic atmosphere of the time encouraged others besides those who lived by crime to disturb the peace. Young men of "good" family formed gangs to roam the streets by night and molest any defenseless person whom they came across; activities of this nature, which seem to have begun in the licentious time of the Restoration, persisted until well into the nineteenth century.

It cannot be said that the government was indifferent to the state of crime, for it resorted to various expedients to detect, repress, and prevent it. King George II asked the houses of Parliament to consider "effectual provisions" against the prevailing robbery and violence. Sir William Mildmay, then resident in Paris, was informed of this, and conscious "that these great evils were happily suppressed, both in the capital, and in all the provinces of France," produced a substantial manuscript report in 1752 for the information of the British government, later amplified and published as a book. The better state of the public peace across the English Channel, though admirable as it was, depended on the regular deployment among the populace of the armed forces, and centrally directed measures, to ensure the salubrity, safety, and provisioning of Paris. Such encroachments on the liberty of the subject (not to mention on the power of local authorities) were almost unthinkable in Georgian England, where the king's power to maintain an army had to be renewed annually by the legislature. The French aphorist Chamfort, writing late in the eighteenth century, quotes a lady who commented that police must indeed be a terrible thing if the English preferred to have thieves and assassins.

The government, therefore, had recourse to other measures. The criminal law was periodically strengthened by making more offenses punishable by death; by the end of the century, there were over two hundred capital crimes. This did not reduce the volume of delinquency, despite the numbers who paid the penalty (Dr. Samuel Johnson wrote satirically that there was scarcely enough rope to supply both the gallows and the navy), largely because there were insufficient peace officers to enforce the law. The severity of punishment was also counterproductive, in that judges and juries sometimes drew back, in an age when a child could be hanged for stealing a handkerchief, from condemning to death persons who had committed what were probably not very serious offenses.

Harsh as the criminal law was, crime had to be proved in open court. In France the royal judges sat in secret, and the king could detain people indefinitely without trial. In England, the writ and act of *habeas corpus* guaranteed a prisoner's right to appear before a judge. The due process of law, however, was subject to many hazards, such as the intimidation of witnesses and the scaring by thieves' attorneys of ignorant constables and unlearned justices of the peace with threats of actions for false imprisonment or malicious prosecution. Much of the onus of prosecution was upon private persons, and these were often discouraged by the expense and trouble of the procedure.

In the absence of effective law-enforcement officers, the government resorted to offering rewards and immunities to those whose information resulted in criminals being prosecuted to conviction. This measure, used increasingly from the last decade of the seventeenth century, resulted in the emergence of a kind of bounty hunters called "thief-takers," often more aptly described as "thief-makers," for many of them found it easier and safer to tempt foolish people into committing felonies than to risk their own lives by going after dangerous offenders. Many of the thief-takers were themselves criminals and, as informers, they were held in great detestation by the British public. The authorities had done little good and much harm by entering, as it were, into partnership with such sinister associates.

Eighteenth-century London had gone so far along the criminal road that organized crime established itself in the form of businesslike and ruthless gangs. The connection of such gangs with thief-taking was particularly evident in the case of Jonathan Wild, self-styled "Thief-Taker General for Great Britain and Northern Ireland."

Thief-taker he was indeed, for he is reputed to have brought some seventy-five felons to justice, and he seems to have lacked neither resourcefulness nor physical courage. His principal activity, though, was even more lucrative: he was England's largest receiver of stolen property that sometimes, at a price, was restored to its owners. He had warehouses in England and Holland, and his own ship. His position as a receiver gave him power over the gangs, and for the first and only time in its history London had a single master of the criminal underworld. Wild's discipline was inflexible, and any thief or robber who held out on Wild the "receiver" found himself in the remorseless grip of Wild the "thief-taker." He ruled the criminal scene from 1714 until 1725, eventually following his felons to the scaffold.

Organized crime did not die with Wild. A quarter of a century after his execution, Henry Fielding denounced what was clearly a "mob" in the American sense:

> What may the public not apprehend, when they are informed as an unquestionable fact, that there are at this time a great gang of rogues, whose number falls little short of a hundred, who are incorporated in one body, have officers and a treasury, and have reduced theft and robbery into a regular system? There are of this society of men who appear in all disguises, and mix in most companies. Nor are they better versed in every art of cheating, thieving, and robbing, than they are armed with every method of evading the law, if they should ever be discovered, and an attempt made to bring them to justice. Here, if they fail in rescuing the prisoner, or (which seldom happens) in bribing or deterring the prosecutor, they have for their last resource some rotten members of the law to forge a defence for them, and a great number of false witnesses ready to support it.

Fielding also recorded that officers of justice with warrants for the arrest of a gangster in their pockets had to pass by, in certain areas, without executing them, being only too well aware that armed members of the same gang were ready to rush to the rescue.

Another expedient on which the government relied heavily in its attempt to control crime was exemplary punishment. It was fervently believed that the spectacle of terrible public retribution was a great deterrent, although the incessant drafts of persons to suffer it did little to substantiate the notion. The public executions at Tyburn, far from striking terror into the hearts of evildoers, were regarded by all and sundry as a kind of Roman holiday. If London's authorities failed to provide bread, they did at least offer circuses, at which people were hanged, decapitated, burned, and disembowelled. Highwaymen had their hour of glory making speeches on their way to the gallows, and, incidentally, the pickpockets did good business.

By this and the other time-honored expedients mentioned

above, the authorities, bemused by ancient slogans of peace keeping and law enforcement, seem to have fed the very fire which they sought to extinguish. Fortunately, amid the blindness and brutality of their century, there were men who had the vision, the intellect, and the character to blaze a better trail.

CHAPTER 3

The Precursors

Bow Street

It was at this grim time for law enforcement and public security that there came what may be termed a "precursive" phase in the development of professional police. As the position was worst in London, it was natural that this phase should begin there. Police reform usually begins as sheer self-defense against the destructive forces of urban disorder and urban crime. This happened in Rome under Augustus Caesar, and in Paris under Louis XIV. In London, however, the reforming impetus did not, as in Rome and Paris, come from the zenith of government. It came from within the obsolescent criminal justice system itself, and its prime movers were a very few exceptional men who held the then much discredited office of justice of the peace.

The landmark of the precursive movement was a justice's court situated in Bow Street, Covent Garden, at that time London's inner-city pleasure district, a little world of theatres, clubs, taverns, gambling houses, and brothels, where licentiousness and money, as always, attracted crime and corruption.

To this scene came Justice Thomas De Veil, who had already made a reputation as a capable and unflinching magistrate in a rough and less sophisticated part of London; he established his court in Bow Street in 1740. Courage and ability are not restricted to the virtuous, and De Veil's biographers refer to his sexual rapacity, and imply that he was, on occasion, corrupt. The facts remain that he made fearless and resourceful attacks on crime and disorder until his death in office in 1746, and that he was the magistrate who gave the Bow Street court its primacy among London's magistrates' courts that it still enjoys.

The most famous of all Bow Street's justices entered his duties there two years later. Henry Fielding (1707–54), remembered by the general public as one of the very greatest English novelists, author of *Tom Jones,* was not very far from the end of his short life when, after seeking to make a living as dramatist, journalist, novelist, advocate, and business man, beset by illness and financial cares, some influential friends came to his aid by engineering his appointment as a magistrate, in the belief that this would provide a haven for a man in distress.

For Fielding it was much more than that. His interest in law and crime was already deep, as a glance at his plays, early novels and other writings shows, and he had practical experience as a lawyer in the London and provincial courts. He was, by birth and character, a gentleman, incorruptible and generous minded, and of the little money he took in fees the greater part went to his clerk. This was made possible because he received some modest remuneration from the government, no doubt in recognition of the value of his advice on criminal policy. This governmental stipend was continued for his successors, and Fielding was thus the first of the "stipendiary" magistrates who still constitute a small but very significant part of Britain's magisterial system.

His attack on crime culminated in operations against gangsters in 1753. Though chronically ill and strongly advised to take sick leave, he canceled all other arrangements in order to respond to an appeal from the government. He was asked no less than to invent a plan to stop the murders and robberies that were rampant in the streets of the capital.

He submitted a scheme, which was approved and funded. It worked on classical lines: he paid "a fellow who had undertaken, for a small sum," to betray the members of the principal gang "into the hands of a set of thief-takers whom I had enlisted into the service, all men of known and approved fidelity and intrepidity." This operation (seven cutthroats in custody, the rest driven away) was successful. Fielding recreates the experience:

> Tho' my health was now reduced to the last extremity, I continued to act with utmost vigour against these villains; in examining whom, and in taking depositions against them, I have often spent whole days, nay sometimes whole nights, especially when there was any difficulty in procuring sufficient evidence to convict them; which is a very common case in street robberies, even when the guilt of the party is sufficiently apparent to satisfy the most tender conscience. But courts of justice know nothing of a cause more than what is told them on oath by a witness; and the most flagitious villain upon earth is tried in the same manner as a man of the best character, who is accused of the same crime.

Plus ça change ....The immediate result of Fielding's operations was:

> That this hellish society were almost utterly extirpated, and that, instead of reading of murders and street-robberies in the news, almost every morning, there was in the remaining part of the month of November, and in all December, not only no such thing as a murder, but not even a street-robbery committed. . . . In this entire freedom from street-robberies, during the dark months, no man will, I believe, scruple to acknowledge that the winter of 1753 stands unrival'd, during a course of many years; and this may possibly appear the more extraordinary to those who recollect the outrages with which it began.

It was not the mere offering of rewards to informers that accounts for the effectiveness of this attack on crime. Fielding gives the clue when he mentions "a set of thief-takers." He had, in fact, founded London's first detective force, to be known in the following century as "the Bow Street Runners," when he invited a few good citizens who had served the office of constable to work under him in the detection of crime. Half a dozen honest, brave men, directed by a magistrate learned in the law, were the first members of a detective force which existed from the mid-eighteenth century until its dissolution in 1839.

During these last few years of his life, Henry Fielding's industry was enormous. He published his two greatest novels, *Tom Jones* (1749) and *Amelia* (1751), concerned himself with the dissemination of crime news through the press, with the aim of interesting and involving the public in crime prevention and detection, and he also wrote what is surely the first criminological treatise in English, in the sense that his purpose was to isolate and describe the *causes* of crime and to propose remedies for them: his *Enquiry into the Causes of the Late Increase of Robbers* (1751). He saw the problem through the eyes of a man of his time and class: the resort of the common people to amusements, drunkenness, and gambling; the uselessness of the existing parochial arrangements for the relief and regulation of the poor; the ease with which stolen property could be disposed of ("if there were no receivers there would be no thieves"), and the general inefficiency of criminal justice. His description is perhaps more valuable than his proposals, but what is remarkable about the *Enquiry* is that its author placed the magistrate's task in its social context, and saw that what has too often, even today, been regarded as a matter for the police is so widely spread and deeply rooted that much more than the agencies of criminal justice are needed to cope with it.

His achievement, striking as it was, might have been ephemeral—only six years in office in which to initiate so much—had it not been that, in addition to his superb eloquence as a writer, he had the inestimable gift of being able to communicate his ideas to others and cause them to share and perpetuate his vision.

One of these was his devoted clerk, Joshua Brogden, whose health was ruined by a working day of almost sixteen hours "in the most unwholesome, as well as nauseous air in the universe." Beyond his duties in court he wrote accounts of Henry's criminal cases for the press. Another was Saunders Welch (1711–84), born into a pauper family and educated in the parish workhouse, who nevertheless became a successful grocer and held office as High Constable of Holborn. He took his law-enforcement responsibilities with exceptional seriousness, and his knowledge of London's underworld, his practicality and dedication earned Henry Fielding's warm regard. The person who built most successfully on Henry's foundations, however, was his half brother, John Fielding (1721–80). John had been blinded in an accident when he was nineteen years of age, a misfortune that he bore with exemplary fortitude, and to which his character and talents enabled him to rise superior. Henry associated John with him in a business enterprise, and secured his appointment as a magistrate in 1751, whereafter he acted as his half-brother's assistant, taking over as principal magistrate at Bow Street when Henry retired in 1754.

John Fielding carried on Henry Fielding's work, notably in strengthening the detective force, "Mr. Fielding's people," in order to continue the attack on violent crime. The security won by Henry's victory had not lasted long: another "desperate" gang soon made its appearance. John and his men renewed the offensive, and in the early months of 1754 organized street robbery was smashed, with more capital offenders brought to justice. (The encounter was a bloody one; a member of the detective force was killed, and a robber was "cut to pieces.") The next target was the highwaymen who infested the approaches to London, and here again the Bow Street men were able to bring enough offenders to justice to discourage the rest.

John then turned his attention to the "numerous Gangs of Housebreakers, Lead and Iron stealers," with similarly good results. Then followed a cleanup of the streets, directed against "the vast shoals of Shop-lifters, Pilferers and Pickpockets," many of whom were caught and sentenced to transportation. This sweep revealed to John a social evil of tragic dimensions, for the offenders

> ... consisted chiefly of Boys from twelve to sixteen Years of Age, either the Children of Thieves or the deserted Offspring of idle and profligate Parents; many of whom, especially Mothers, shamefully subsisted from their Robberies: And what was very remarkable, four infant Thieves, the oldest of whom was but five years of Age, were brought before John Fielding, which appeared to be Children of different Persons, collected together by one Woman to beg and steal to furnish that Beast with Gin.

Nearly a hundred years later, Charles Dickens found such exploitation of children still rife and exposed it in his magazine serial, *Oliver Twist* (1837–38).

Here (if anywhere) was a crying need for prevention, and John Fielding was not slow to seek preventive measures. His first step was to provide an alternative way of life for the juvenile street criminals, by sending them to sea as servants in the Royal Navy. The idea found favor and subscriptions came in to fund it; subsequently, the scheme was institutionalized and became the Marine Society. By 1758, since its inception in 1756, 2,405 boys were clothed and taken aboard the king's ships, and over 3,000 young men were fitted out to be enlisted in the Navy.

Fielding's concern extended, *inter alia,* to the female counterparts of the young thieves ("And as these deserted Boys were Thieves from Necessity, their Sisters are Whores for the same Cause"); the measures he proposed were adopted, and from them developed the Magdalen Hospital and the Female Orphan Asylum. He had inherited Henry's profound social commitment, and in the ampler sphere accorded him, had given it not only wide but also lasting, practical application: all three of the above charities have survived into the twentieth century.

Such police patrolling as there was before John Fielding's day was done at night, by the watchmen, and though one cannot accept the wholesale verdict that the watch was corrupt, decrepit, and worse than useless, it is clear that the parochial limits and the night stint would have limited the effectiveness even of better-manned systems. Fielding first put out a couple of mounted patrolmen, but in 1763 he received government funding for a horse patrol of ten men, to operate on London's suburban perimeter. The detective and preventive efficacy of the horse patrol was proved within a year, but then the government cut off the funds and he had to make do as best he could with two horsemen and his Bow Street "people" for the remainder of his time in office.

Like Henry Fielding, John had great faith in the press as an agent to counter crime and he did everything in his power to publicize the proceedings of his court. It was in his time that Bow Street, as envisaged by Henry, became fully established as a court, open to the public, as distinct from the usual court held at a magistrate's private premises, where proceedings were virtually *in camera.* John encouraged victims of crime to come to him. He published information sheets, showing how thieves attacked property. He is, indeed, the apostle of police-public relations.*

---

*See Anthony Babington, *A House in Bow Street,* p. 86.

John Fielding realized, too, that crime could not be fought successfully within narrow territorial limits; he had found, and modern police administrators often have had occasion to re-learn the lesson, that it is necessary to give out and attract information about crime and criminals. To this end, he built up a correspondence with magistrates elsewhere, often outside London, and he must rank as the pioneer of systematic communication of criminal information. In 1772 he founded two police newspapers, *The Quarterly Pursuit,* and *The Weekly* or *Extraordinary Pursuit,* to be sent free of charge to justices at large, in which were printed lists and particulars of "wanted" criminals and of criminal offenses. From these publications eventually evolved the *Police Gazette,* founded in 1828 and published since 1883 by New Scotland Yard.

John Fielding received the honor of knighthood in 1761, and this fittingly symbolizes the enduring nature of his achievements: his successors as chief magistrate at Bow Street have all been similarly honored. His contribution to police development was immense. He confirmed the value of a detective branch, demonstrated the value of patrolling, exploited the crime preventive capacity of the press, and never lost sight of the social context of crime. His ideas on further reform continued to germinate after his death. It is fitting that he should have been the first person to make regular use in English of the term "police" in its law-enforcement sense today.

Public Disorder

One of the hard facts that confronted the government in the eighteenth century was that its resources for the maintenance of public order were dangerously insufficient. It was an age of riots, and though such energetic justices as De Veil and the Fieldings were able to quell several outbreaks, the evil remained, sporadically erupting, ever threatening, until well into the following century. Public disorder is perhaps the gravest of the problems that beset police authorities and police executives in all ages.

Sir John Fielding was on his deathbed in his house outside London when the worst riot in the whole of London's modern history broke out.

Public turbulence in the eighteenth century was generated by political, economic, and religious causes. The Gordon Riots in 1780 began in protest against Parliament's recent relaxation of the repressive legislation against Roman Catholics. Extreme Protestants, incensed by this, persuaded a young Scottish nobleman, Lord George Gordon, to lead a march on the legislature and present a monster petition for repeal of the laws in question.

Some fifty thousand people assembled on Friday, June 2d, wearing blue cockades, and began to march in an orderly way towards the houses of Parliament. En route, however, they were joined by persons of a wilder and more predatory kind, the perennial elements of the London mob. The approaches to Parliament were soon choked, and when peers and members of the House of Commons arrived that afternoon they were savagely manhandled and had to fight their way into the chambers.

The insufficiency of the civil power was apparent immediately, and remained so for the duration of the emergency. Two justices and half a dozen constables could not disperse this violent mob, several thousand strong, and only when units of cavalry and infantry were brought up by two other justices could the situation be even barely stabilized. The crowd melted away by 10:00 P.M. and it seemed that the trouble was over.

At midnight, however, wrecking crews, amply provided with axes, hammers, spades, and crowbars, attacked the chapels of the Sardinian and Bavarian embassies, both representatives of Roman Catholic states, smashing windows, and stripping furnishings and making bonfires of them in the streets. Troops ordered to the scene stood by and watched: it was firmly fixed in the military mind that soldiers could not open fire without orders from a civil magistrate, and civil magistrates were in exceedingly short supply during the Gordon Riots.

Saturday was a quiet day, but at at 9:00 P.M. there began a furious attack on the quarter where Irish laborers had settled in doss-houses and shanties; their offense was not so much that they were Roman Catholics as that they worked, as poor immigrants always will, for far less than the native workers demanded. This area remained under attack for over two days, all chapels being burned, houses broken into, and looting rife. The troops again proved useless, insisting on magisterial orders that were never given.

Tuesday night saw the sacking and burning of an unpopular

justice's house, the storming of London's major prison, Newgate, the release of hundreds of prisoners, the stripping of furnishings from Sir John Fielding's house on Bow Street, the sacking and burning of the house of the Lord Chief Justice of England, and the breaking open of three more prisons. At last a justice gave the soldiers orders to fire on a mob in one of London's squares. The authorities were plucking up their courage, having summoned troops and militia to come in by forced marches from all over the country.

Chaos was everywhere, people lying dead drunk among smoldering ashes in the streets, houses windowless, walls broken and blackened. Groups of predators were looting and extorting money from all and sundry, and more substantial mischief was to be feared.

King George III called his privy council and demanded a legal ruling on whether the army could only open fire if ordered by a civil magistrate. The attorney-general said that army officers legally had discretion to fire on a mob to prevent the commission of felonies. This was immediately communicated to the officers. By now the government had concentrated some fifteen thousand troops and militia in London, and vulnerable points, public and private, were now under guard.

That Wednesday night, nevertheless, saw the sky lighted red with the fires from three more prisons and the mob seizure of a large distillery, with gin-maddened rioters, people poisoned by the raw spirits, and burned to death in flaming alcohol. There were three fierce attacks on the Bank of England, some of the assailants having firearms; there were repelled by musket fire and cavalry charges.

Thursday and Friday saw comparative calm, but it was widely reported that the military were trying and executing captured rioters. Saturday saw the end of the emergency, and there was general rejoicing.

The Gordon Riots remain something of a mystery. The orchestration of the attacks, the later concentration on action against the symbols of law enforcement, the uprising's limitation of its onslaught to property—the rioters killed no one; the killing was done by the authorities. Interpretations of the turbulence of June 1780 included, as those of such events usually do, the notion that international mischief, the work of Britain's foes, was at the root of it all, but there is little evidence for this. More probable was the idea of the culpability of persons whose international trade had suffered as a result of the American war, but this was not substantiated. It is likeliest of all that the riots began as a legitimate protest by a section of the public, and then flared into a general uprising of the criminal and deprived against authority and the privileged classes. The pent-up misery of the great city burst its bounds and had its week of anarchical rage.

The failure of the civil power was much censured, but so was the government's use of military force. Charles James Fox, a leader of the parliamentary opposition, declared that he "would rather be governed by a mob than a standing army." It seemed that the obdurate British valued liberty far above order. Had the hundreds of people killed, the property destroyed, and the protracted disruption of the life of the capital taught them nothing?

Progress

For a moment it seemed that the authorities had come to their senses. In 1785, obviously mindful of their eclipse in the previous year, the government, now headed by William Pitt the Younger, brought a bill to the House of Commons that proposed to create a system of magistrates' courts along the Bow Street model, and also a single police force, under three commissioners, for the cities of London and Westminster and contiguous areas. This bill aroused so much opposition on the part of the existing order, especially in the powerful City of London, that it had to be withdrawn. The loss was not total, as the scheme was put into effect the following year in the capital of Ireland by the Dublin Police Act.

The thirty-two-year span of the Fieldings' tenure at Bow Street had nevertheless firmly established the principle of a salaried magistracy, superior in standard, consistency, and openness of jurisdiction, and in 1792 Pitt returned to magisterial reform. This time his bill passed into law as: "An Act for the more effectual administration of the office of a Justice of the Peace in such parts of the counties of Middlesex and Surrey as lie in and near the Metropolis, and for the more effectual prevention of felonies."

This act established seven police courts, in addition to Bow

Street, at each of which would sit three stipendiary magistrates. The police provisions of the law concerned the appointment of six constables at each of these courts, and the conferring of limited power for constables to make arrests on suspicion.

Meanwhile, John Fielding's successor at Bow Street, Sir Sampson Wright, was following up John's ideas on patrol. He revived the horse patrol for the London approaches and instituted a foot patrol for the streets. Thus he had, as it were, both a detective branch (the "runners") and a patrol force, though neither was ever numerous enough for the task before it.

One of the principal benefits of the 1792 act was the appointment of an exceptional man as one of the new stipendiary justices. Patrick Colquhoun (1745–1820) was a transatlantic trader and a former Lord Provost (chief magistrate) of the city of Glasgow, Scotland. He stands in direct line with the Fieldings, to whose "excellent ideas and accurate and extensive knowledge upon every subject connected with the Police of the Metropolis," as he put it, he paid handsome tribute. Colquhoun was closely associated with the philosopher Jeremy Bentham (1738–1832), whose ideal system of jurisprudence emphasized the necessity for preventive police.

Like the Fieldings, Colquhoun was deeply aware of London's social miseries. He was not afraid to use force when force was unavoidable—pistol in hand, he faced armed rioters on occasion—but he was much more concerned with the alleviation of distress than with the repression of its consequences. Many thousands of destitute were fed at the soup kitchens he opened; many a workman was able to redeem the tools of his trade from the pawnbroker with money that Colquhoun had collected for that purpose. Like his great predecessors, too, he used the printed word to spread his ideas and record his activities. Two of his books are police classics.

A Treatise on the Police of the Metropolis (1795) reflects his consciousness of being in the forefront of a great social and administrative development, as when he writes:

> Police in this Country may be considered as a *new Science;* the properties of which consist not in the Judicial Powers which lead to Punishment, and which belong to Magistrates alone; but in the PREVENTION and DETECTION OF CRIMES, and in those other Functions

which relate to INTERNAL REGULATIONS for the well ordering and comfort of Civil Society.

There was the formula: prevention was given pride of place above detection.

Colquhoun's study and exposition of London's police arrangements led him to urge that there should be central coordination and direction, not only for London but for the whole country. This was too much for the authorities; they considered his ideas, and drew back. His argument was attractive:

> ...Let it once become the duty of one body of men to charge themselves with the execution of the Laws, for the prevention of crimes, and the detection of offences—let them be armed with proper and apposite powers for that purpose, and the state of Society will speedily become ameliorated and improved; a greater degree of security will be extended to the peaceful subject, and the blessings of civil liberty will be enlarged.

History would vindicate him.

Businessman and magistrate, Colquhoun's practicality and respect for the law are evident throughout his two great books; the second, *The Commerce and Police of the River Thames* (1800), tells the story of a successful police venture into crime prevention. It presents a remarkable account of crime and its modes of operation on London's river and waterfront, then the world's busiest and richest port, with exports and imports valued at that time at thirty million pounds. His appreciation showed that crime had become a way of life among the port labor force and a rich source of profit for the receivers who handled the stolen goods. He called it "a monstrous System of Depredation," but he had the sense of proportion to know that this species of theft was very different from burglary and robbery, and he believed it could be greatly reduced by preventive policing.

His belief was put to the acid test. Colquhoun and John Harriott (1745–1817) had put forward a scheme that involved the establishment of a new magistrate's court, with clerks and constables, a preventive police branch to supervise and patrol the river and the wharves, and arrange for ship guards, and a branch to control the employment of dock labor so as to engage men of good character and ensure that the contractors paid their people, as opposed to the prevailing system of letting them steal to make their living. The Committee of the West India Merchants, principal sufferers from the thieves, and the government, partner in the merchants' troubles by reason of lost customs dues, agreed to finance the scheme jointly. The business of organization and recruitment went forward rapidly, and the Thames police came into operation in 1799.

Colquhoun had the invaluable cooperation throughout of Harriott, a former naval and army officer, who assumed the day-to-day conduct of the court and served as commander of the preventive police. He was resident magistrate and Colquhoun supervising magistrate, and their steady and humane administration, after some violent and bloody opposition from the work force, soon established the enterprise.

The early success of the Thames police was spectacular. The West India Merchants reckoned that in the police's first eight months, losses from theft were reduced by ninety-five percent. The government was so favorably impressed that the scheme (minus the dock labor branch) was taken over as a wholly public responsibility in 1800. Colquhoun had proved that the presence of a disciplined police, in contrast to that of shabby watchmen, was an effective means of preventing crime. In 1839, his river police became the Thames Division of the Metropolitan Police.

Repression

The century drawing to an end and the early decades of its successor were deeply disturbed by war and the aftermath of war, and the fear of wholesale insurrection. The government, at war with first revolutionary and then Napoleonic France (1793–1815) had to face the dangers of espionage and subversion, as well as large-scale political and economic disorder in both Great Britain and Ireland.

The magistrates, especially at Bow Street, found themselves engaged in counterespionage and the arrest of revolutionary conspirators at the behest of the central government, the ministry

concerned being the home office, where systematic policing of
aliens had made a firm beginning.*

To have brought an adequate civil police system into being at
this distracted time was certainly beyond the political capacity of
the authorities, not to mention the logistics of such a measure.
They therefore relied on military force and domestic spies. The
war and the dislocation caused by new manufacturing methods
fomented industrial discontent: old crafts were obsolescent;
mechanical innovations were putting people out of work. Machinery was smashed. There was a surging movement for reform of the
hopelessly inequitable electoral system and for trade unions to
protect employees.

Magistrates augmented the constabulary by swearing in
special constables (which an act of Parliament of 1668 empowered
them to do), but the great resource to safeguard industrial property
and contain public turbulence was the soldiers—the regular army,
far too small for widespread civil defense, the militia, and the vol-
unteer regiments, drawn from the local propertied classes, known
as the yeomanry; this auxiliary force had been embodied during
the threat of Napoleonic invasion but was to see action only in order maintenance.

Lord Sidmouth, who became home secretary in 1812, strug-
gling against the tide of near revolutionary violence, used to the
full both the military and his ministry's rapidly developed intelligence resources in the form of spies and informers. The criminal courts hanged and transported; the soldiers fired and charged;
and, focal as the Gordon Riots had been in 1780, there occurred in
1819 the confrontation which passed into history as the Peterloo
Massacre.

This was precipitated by a huge political meeting in St. Peter's
Fields, Manchester—principal industrial city of northern England—where those militating for economic relief and parliamentary reform were united by the influence of nonconformist Protes-
tantism, the Methodism to which the French historian Halévy at-
tributed England's abstention from revolution in the nineteenth
century. Those who mustered in St. Peter's Fields on August 16,
1819, were in no mood for riot, let alone revolution. Women and

*See Roger Wells, *Insurrection*, pp. 28–43.

children were present in great numbers among the sixty thousand people who had come to listen to a famous radical orator, Henry Hunt, on the subject of parliamentary reform.

The magistrates on the scene decided that Hunt and his committee should be arrested, thinking that this would cause the meeting to disperse. Hunt and his colleagues, however, were surrounded on their platform by the dense multitude, and the constables saw no way in which they, unaided, could serve the magistrates' warrants. The justices, therefore, called in the military. A troop of yeomanry cavalry rode into the crowd; their first victim was a two-year-old child, killed in the onrush. The yeomanry had been carousing, and this, with their poor discipline and untrained mounts, caused them to lose formation and founder in the press of people. The platform was reached nevertheless, and the arrests were made.

At this point the amateur soldiers, overexcited by their success, lost their heads and began smashing the dais and dragging down the banners. The magistrates, too far off to make out what was happening, concluded that the crowd was attacking the yeomanry. They ordered a newly arrived contingent of regular cavalry to disperse the gathering. Their charge created panic and people fled as best they could, leaving sabered and trampled bodies on the ground. Fifteen died; several hundred were wounded or injured.

The bitter sobriquet of "Peterloo" (a word play on St. Peter's Fields and Waterloo) became irrevocably attached to the event, and it was spoken of as a massacre. In the longer term it would be seen as a monument on the road to the great Reform Act of 1832, but in the short term, despite the severe shock to civilized public opinion, the government pursued its repressive policy. The magistrates were fulsomely praised; Hunt and others were sentenced to prison terms for unlawful assembly; Parliament hastily passed legislation giving emergency powers in connection with search, seizure, and arrest, the banning of public meetings, and the suppression of inflammatory writings. The army recruited another ten thousand men. Outbreaks of rioting, which occurred all over the country, were speedily enveloped by troops; there were some capital sentences and the transportation of several hundred convicts. Lord Sidmouth remained home secretary until 1822, when a new prime minister, Lord Liverpool, appointed Robert Peel to succeed him.

Peel (1788–1850) was no stranger to public turbulence. Chief Secretary (principal administrator) of Ireland from 1812 to 1818, he had seen a country with wretched peace keeping machinery ravaged by rioting which could only be put down by the use of such troops as could be spared from Britain's war with Napoleon. He therefore brought into being a new kind of civil police. The Peace Preservation Act of 1814 provided for the Lord Lieutenant of Ireland to establish police in any area in which he saw fit to proclaim a state of disturbance. Recruitment was from ex-military men and the Peace Preservation Force enjoyed some early success.

The new home secretary soon found himself up against the apparently unshakable British dogma that police spelt tyranny. He appointed a parliamentary committee under his own chairmanship to consider police reform, but the committee reported in 1823, in an oft-quoted passage:

> It is difficult to reconcile an effective system of police with that perfect freedom of action and exemption from interference, which are the great privileges and blessings in this country; and your Committee think that the forfeiture or curtailment of such advantages would be too great a sacrifice for improvements in police, or facilities in detection of crime.

Six years later, John Wade spoke up for the British way:

> ... We have no *espionnage* corps for mingling in social intercourse; we have no registry-office for recording the name, abode, and occupation of every inhabitant; nor have we any barriers round the metropolis at which every stranger may be arrested, measured, and catalogued before he can enter its boundaries. These precautions may be necessary in some countries; but, numerous and flagrant as are the delinquencies of London, we are very far from having attained that pitch of general depravity which renders such encroachments on individual freedom essential to public safety.*

Peel bided his time. He had already succeeded in having Parliament enact much needed reform of the criminal law. Police im-

*A Treatise on the Police and Crimes of the Metropolis, 1829, p. 62.

provement was not beyond his capacity. The moment came when the Duke of Wellington, victor of Waterloo, became prime minister in 1828. The duke had strong views on the police problem; the greatest living British soldier had little confidence in soldiers as peace keepers and was well aware of the peril of a state which had to rely on its army to maintain order. There had been mutiny and there was disaffection, even in the Guards regiments; in 1823, Wellington had told Lord Liverpool that measures should be taken immediately "to form either a police in London or a military corps, which should be of a different description from the regular military force, or both." There the matter had rested, but when Wellington succeeded as prime minister, police reform was given fresh impetus. Peel appointed another committee, also in 1828, and this time the members concluded that it was "absolutely necessary to devise some means to give greater security to persons and property." This gave Peel his opportunity. He set the legislative process in motion.

CHAPTER 4

The New Police

The Metropolitan Police Act of 1829

The police system that Peel had committed himself to reform was not as despicable as some writers have assumed. The Bow Street magistracy at this time had under its direction the detective branch (8 runners) and 4 patrol forces (some 350 men in all), 1 of which operated by day. The 7 magistrates' offices, created in 1792, each had upwards of 6 constables to function, *inter alia*, as detectives. Colquhoun's river police numbered about 90, plus a dock watch of 67. The City of London had 57 police officers. The parochial police for the whole London area had 3,659 parish constables (many serving by deputy) and parish watchmen.* The central government paid for the police establishments of Bow Street, the 1792 magistrates' courts, and the river. The City of London paid for its police officers. The parochial police were financed by the local tax raised by the authorities of each parish.

The heterogeneity and negative features of the system are at-

*John Wade, *A Treatise on the Police and Crimes of the Metropolis*, 1829, p. 64.

tacked in the preamble of Peel's great Act for improving the Police in and near the Metropolis:

> Whereas Offences against Property have of late increased in and near the Metropolis; and the local Establishments of Nightly Watch and Nightly Police have been found inadequate to the Prevention and Detection of Crime, by reason of the frequent Unfitness of the individuals employed, the Insufficiency of their Number, the limited Sphere of their Authority, and their want of Connection and Co-operation with each other; and whereas it is expedient to substitute a new and more efficient System of Police in lieu of such Establishments of Nightly Watch and Nightly Police, within the limits hereinafter mentioned, and to constitute an Office of Police, which, acting under the immediate Authority of One of His Majesty's Principal Secretaries of State, shall direct and control the whole of such new System of Police.

The bill had passed into law, without opposition. Peel, with political finesse, had respected the independence of the City of London by not including it in the area of the act's jurisdiction, which was called the Metropolitan Police District. The City of London still has its own police force.

The Act provided for a single police system to be established for that district, under the supervision of two justices of the peace who would be answerable to the secretary of state, i.e., the home secretary. These justices would not perform judicial duties: their business was "the Preservation of the Peace, the Prevention of Crimes, the Detection and Committal of Offenders." They were to be not "judicial" justices but "administrative" justices. Soon they would be known as "Commissioners of Police of the Metropolis." One of their duties would be to appoint and swear in constables.

It is a cardinal feature of the Metropolitan Police Act of 1829 that the police force was to consist of "constables," thus giving this most ancient of Common Law offices a new lease of life. The constable's oath prescribed service to the crown and the performance of duty according to law.* Individually responsible for his actions,

---

*Today the constable makes a declaration, as follows: "... I will well and truly serve our Sovereign Lady the Queen in the office of constable, without favour or affection, malice or ill-will; and that I will to the best of my power cause the peace to be kept and preserved, and prevent all offences against the persons and

he could not plead obedience to orders from superiors if he acted illegally. His authority was original and derived from the Common Law. He would, nevertheless be a member of a disciplined body, and as such subject to the direction of superiors.

The commissioners were to have command of the force, but for its business administration another official, the Receiver for the Metropolitan Police, was to answer to the home secretary. The collection of the local taxes previously applied to the parochial police would be his hardest task, but the buildings, equipment, and property of the force also were part of his accountability.

Preparations

Robert Peel cast about to find the three men who would fill the three top posts. A retired lieutenant-colonel, Charles Rowan, a veteran of Waterloo, where he had fought (and been badly wounded) with the 52nd Light Infantry, with line and staff experience gained in the Peninsular War, was the first of the two commissioners to be appointed. The second was a lawyer, Richard Mayne, a practicing advocate. The receiver's post was filled by John Wray, also an advocate.

The Metropolitan Police Act had become law on June 19, 1829, and the summer of that year was spent in preparations to put it into operation.

Peel was determined to keep the force clear of any political control except his own, which was statutory, and in that age, when "jobbery" was the general rule in the public service, he succeeded remarkably in ensuring that the constables and ranking members of the force were not accepted for appointment merely because influential people had recommended them.

It was decided that the force should wear uniform, but care was taken to avoid a military appearance. The main features of the prescribed dress were a blue swallow-tailed coat, a leather stock,

---

properties of her Majesty's subjects; and that while I continue to hold the said office I will to the best of my skill and knowledge discharge all the duties thereof faithfully according to law." (Police Act of 1964)

and a reinforced top hat. A rattle was carried, to give the alarm and summon help.* The collar of the coat showed a letter indicating to which division the constable belonged, followed by his personal number.

There were thousands of applications to join the force. Some were from ex-soldiers, but most were made by laborers. Peel wanted his police to be representative of the largest section of British society. There was a deterrent, however, built into the scheme, to the recruitment of the better workers: this was the low wage upon which Peel (a rich man, and the son of a rich man, with all the strange perspectives on money to which the wealthy are prone, although the chronic parsimony of government and the difficulty of collecting the local taxes may have been factors) adamantly insisted. A constable's wage was much lower than an artisan's, and for three shillings a day Peel expected to recruit fit men, under thirty-five years of age, literate, and of good character. His obduracy on this point would produce an endless problem of finding and keeping the right men.

Peel also ordained that the divisional superintendents and the inspectors should be former military warrant or noncommissioned officers; he believed that "gentlemen—commissioned officers, for instance . . . would be above their work." This theory would give the police a lower-class stereotype in the public mind, which mid-twentieth century police reformers would find very difficult to change when they strove to recruit the better-educated young people. It may, however, have helped to make the new police more acceptable to the middle and upper classes.

In view of the frequency with which the military model of police has been debated in recent times, it is apposite to emphasize that for all its unarmed and civil style, the Metropolitan Police was built on military lines. The use of military titles was avoided, except for the rank of sergeant, but the standard of discipline and inspection was military. It would often be necessary for the police to march and act in large groups, and it was logical for Peel to look to the armed services for his command and super-

---

*The rattle was replaced by a whistle in 1846, and the top hat by a helmet in 1864.

visory ranks. No one else had anything like as much experience of handling such numbers of men.

Headquarters was established in a house, No. 4, Whitehall Place, adjacent to a court known as Scotland Yard. Thus, from the outset, the force was associated with this now world famous address.*

The Metropolitan Police District, with a population of some two million, was split up into areas, to each of which would be allocated a division, under a superintendent, with lower formations under four inspectors, each inspector having four sergeants under him, and under each sergeant nine constables. The area was divided into "beats," to be patrolled by constables throughout the twenty-four hours; a beat was laid out so that a constable should be able to see every part of it once every fifteen minutes. The 1829 territory of the Metropolitan Police was relatively small, within a radius of four to seven miles from Charing Cross; ten years later it was expanded to a fifteen to sixteen mile radius, approximately its present size.

The "new police" presented an unarmed appearance; the only weapon issued routinely was a wooden truncheon, carried in the swallowtails. Inspectors might carry pocket pistols; pistols and cutlasses were kept in police stations.

General Instructions

The General Instructions issued to the Metropolitan Police in 1829 remain in force. It is probable that the soldier Rowan wrote the first part, dealing with the aims and conduct of the organization, the lawyer Mayne, the second (legal) part, and that Robert Peel annotated the proof copy. Some extracts will show their perennial validity.

> It should be understood, at the outset, that the principal object to be attained is *the Prevention of Crime.*
> To this great end every effort of the Police is to be directed. The

---

*The headquarters moved in 1885 to a building on the Thames Embankment, called New Scotland Yard, and thence in 1967 to another new building off Victoria Street, retaining the name of New Scotland Yard.

security of person and property, the preservation of the public tranquility, and all the other objects of a Police Establishment, will thus be better effected than by the detection and punishment of the offender, after he has succeeded in committing the crime.

Perhaps the most interesting passages of the original instructions are those addressed to the constable, upon whom so much would depend, then as now, and upon whose relationship with the public the whole police edifice rests:

He will be civil and attentive to all persons of every rank and class; insolence or incivility will not be passed over.

... He must be particularly cautious, not to interfere idly or unnecessarily; when required to act, he will do so with decision and boldness; on all occasions he may expect to receive the fullest support in the execution of his authority.

He must remember, that there is no qualification more indispensable to a Police Officer, than a perfect command of temper,* never suffering himself to be moved in the slightest degree, by any language or threats that may be used; if he do his duty in a quiet and determined manner, such conduct will probably induce well-disposed by-standers to assist him, should he require it.

The General Instructions of 1829 are a profoundly influential document in the history of police management. They were issued in booklet form to the force, so that each man knew where he stood—in itself an exemplary feature. They also contained the legal knowledge that was likeliest to be needed by constables, such as that relating to their powers of arrest. Surely, however, the most significant "management" provision was the career prospect offered to the service:

Every Police Constable in the Force may hope to rise by activity, intelligence, and good conduct, to the superior stations. He must make it his study to recommend himself to notice by a diligent discharge of

---

*The Regulations for the Day and Night Police of the City of New York, issued on the institution of the force by Mayor W.F. Havemeyer on July 16, 1845, state (Section 1, paragraph 5): "Members of the department must be civil and respectful to the public, and, upon all occasions, execute their duty with good temper and discretion. No qualification is more indispensable to a policeman than a perfect command of temper; a manly forbearance under provocation, and a temperate, though firm, deportment, will ensure him support in the discharge of his duty...."

his duties, and strict obedience to the commands of his superiors, recollecting that he who has been accustomed to discipline, will be considered best qualified to command.

By the "superior stations," the instructions were referring to the ranks of sergeant, inspector, and superintendent. Posts above superintendent, as they were gradually created, were generally filled from outside the service. It would not be until after the Second World War that a constable would rise to the post of commissioner.

The incentive was, nevertheless, great. It was a sure way of developing cohesiveness within the force, but it also insulated it from outside influences and induced a conservatism that sometimes had unhappy effects. The gods do not give with both hands.

Survival

A memorable exchange of letters took place in November 1829 between Wellington and Peel:*

"I congratulate you on the entire success of the Police in London, it is impossible to see anything more respectable than they are." Peel replied, "I am very glad indeed to hear that you think well of the Police. It has given me from first to last more trouble than anything I ever undertook. But the men are gaining a knowledge of their duties so rapidly, that I am very sanguine of the ultimate result. I want to teach people that liberty does not consist in having your house robbed by organised gangs of thieves, and in leaving the principal streets of London in the nightly possession of drunken women and vagabonds."

Astonishing progress was made in those early months. By June 1830, the force had recruited 17 superintendents, 68 inspectors, 323 sergeants, and 2,906 constables, every one of whom had been interviewed by the commissioners before appointment. The Metropolitan Police District had been split up into 17 divisions, policing a population of almost 1,250,000; police premises had been

*Quoted by W.L. Melville Lee in *A History of Police in England,* p. 243, from C.S. Parker's biography of Peel.

found for divisional stations; uniform and equipment had been issued. A Select Committee of the House of Commons would report in 1834 that losses from robbery with violence and theft had dropped from an annual rate of 900,000 pounds a year to 20,000 pounds. These were estimated figures but the disparity between 1829 and 1834 must have been very great. The police presence in the streets and the collection and communication of criminal intelligence surely account for such success.

While Peel and Wellington were expressing their gratification, however, the force was under several kinds of attack. The pundits of the old order disliked and feared the new power which had arisen in their midst. The stipendiary magistrates at Bow Street and elsewhere stood on their dignity, determined to preserve their police functions, both as regarded public order and crime, and they placed every obstacle in the way of commissioners and constables alike, harassing police officers acting as prosecutors, or appearing as witnesses, and using their political influence to discourage and discredit the police leadership. The parochial authorities smarted under the loss of their ancient police system, and made difficulties over raising and paying the local police tax.

Gravest, perhaps, was the precarious relationship of the commissioners with their political masters. The government of which Peel was a member went out of office in November 1830, leaving many difficult questions undecided, and the home secretaries who succeeded him, first Lord Melbourne, then Viscount Duncannon, were hostile to their predecessor's police. Their conduct, maybe reflecting some obscure notion of "divide and rule" by playing the stipendiary magistrates against the commissioners, seems to have been calculated to induce Rowan and Mayne to resign. Poignant indeed must have been the moments when these two supremely able and honorable men bowed to unseemly ministerial instructions to preserve their larger loyalty to the force which they had brought into action, and which, if they abandoned it, would most probably not survive. Their united fortitude and perfect partnership is a striking example of the capital contribution the character of individuals can make to the development of an institution.*

*Charles Reith's *A New Study of Police History* gives a documented account of these difficult years.

In the streets, the patience and courage of the patrolling officers was taxed to the utmost by abuse and violence: soldiers pitched in to fight these wearers of an alien uniform; firemen fought them for possession of the scenes of fire; coachmen lashed them in defiance of traffic directions. And in the streets, especially at night, a more insidious foe lay in wait: the free drink offered to men who were members of a class which had been prone to alcoholism for over a century. The commissioners faced the problems of police conduct squarely. They would not relax their discipline, and they had supervisors who were seasoned experts in keeping the British soldier in line; the unending business of firing and hiring was done unsparingly. Between 1830 and 1838 there would be five thousand dismissals and over six thousand resignations, drunkenness on duty being a prime cause of dismissal, and the move to better paid and less onerous work, of resignation.

The main physical threat to the force came from the extreme left of the political spectrum. The Ultra-Radicals, themselves neither numerous nor prominent, were desperately bent on creating the anarchical confusion from which revolution might come. They worked on the feelings of the National Political Union of the Working Classes, a more moderate group, in order to provide themselves with the necessary crowds to produce large-scale disorder. To this end, they concentrated their attack on the police, "Peel's Bloody Gang," attributing to them all manner of evil designs as instruments of the government tyranny Britain had always resisted. During their first four years, the Metropolitan Police served their harsh pupilage to the art of order maintenance.

Mob violence, usually politically inspired, sometimes aimed directly at the police, was recurrent. The technique of the baton charge and the value of compact formation were learned as some key confrontations took place, not always handled successfully, but the great Reform Act of 1832, extending the parliamentary franchise, was passed without undue turbulence. Opposition to the police, however, still smoldered.

Fuel was added to the fire when it was discovered that a police sergeant, William Popay, who had been employed in plain clothes to report on meetings of the militants, had exceeded his instructions to the extent of posing as a revolutionary. A radical comrade recognized him in a police station and denounced him. This would lead to a parliamentary inquiry that, in 1834, found Popay's actions "highly reprehensible," and deprecated "any approach to the Employment of Spies" as unacceptable to the public and "most Alien to the spirit of the Constitution."

Meanwhile, the Ultra-Radicals, mobilizing the National Political Union, determined to bring the police to a conclusive battle. They distributed inflammatory notices of a meeting to be held on May 13, 1833.

A piece of wasteland called Cold Bath Fields, in Clerkenwell, and the streets opening into it, were the scene of the struggle. A crowd of some eight hundred people, peaceable at first but soon excited by subversive oratory, fiercely opposed the police when they moved forward to disperse them. Bludgeons, knives, pointed weapons, even pistols were observed, and bricks and stones were thrown. Colonel Rowan, in command, used one police formation of seventy men, with other formations in ample support. Three officers were stabbed, one of whom, Constable Robert Culley, died on the spot. Many police were injured. The savage melee lasted less than ten minutes, and the crowd fled, pursued with understandable anger by truncheon-wielding policemen.

It seemed at first to have been a Pyrrhic victory, such was the vituperation of the police by the local public and the press. A coroner's jury found Constable Culley's murder to have been "justifiable homicide," a fantastically perverse verdict which was reversed by a higher court. A Select Committee of the House of Commons was appointed to inquire into the conduct of the police.

The committee exonerated the commissioners and the force, finding their actions within the law and the execution of the operation proper, save for the pursuit at the end of fugitives by some policemen acting individually. Colonel Rowan, however, had ordered "no violence" (and punished transgression by dismissal). No member of the public was killed, and despite a spate of complaints of police violence, none of these said to have suffered from it came forward to testify. The death of Constable Culley was followed by an unexpected surge of public sympathy for his widow, and subscriptions poured in. The aftermath of the Cold Bath Fields riot saw the police accepted by the majority of citizens.

By the end of the force's first decade, the place of the "new police" in London's life was secure. The intransigent City of London provided itself with a force on the model of the Metropolitan Police. Colquhoun's river police became the Metropolitan Police's Thames Division. Bow Street and the other stipendiary magistracies were deprived of their police officers—even the legendary Bow Street Runners were disbanded. The magistrates' struggle to hang on to their executive police powers was over: London's public order was now firmly in the hands of the Metropolitan Police.

It had been proved that disciplined constables, armed only with truncheons, could master armed mobs, and that the former recourse to the military was no longer necessary. And when the word "police" was used henceforth in Britain, its sense had passed from classical abstract, "internal governance," to something much more immediate: "police" now meant "police officers."

CHAPTER 5

Police Development in the Nineteenth Century

Police Reform in the Provinces

While the fear of political revolution beset the propertied classes, the fact of another revolution became increasingly evident in Britain. Mills, factories, workshops, mines, canals, railways, foundries, were drawing people from their immemorial labor on the land, uprooting them from the villages where everyone knew everyone, and absorbing them in grim towns where all were strangers. As the Industrial Revolution gathered momentum, the population more than doubled in eighty years: by 1830 it had reached fourteen million. These numbers—these new concentrations—put an intolerable strain on local governments as pressing problems of sustenance, poverty, health, and law and order accumulated.

During the half century that followed the Metropolitan Police Act of 1829, legislation promoted by the central government brought great changes in the policing of the country at large. Political reform was the prime motive of the Municipal Corporations Act of 1835, a measure designed to give a voice in local government to the urban middle class. Municipal councils were to be

47

elected on a wider franchise, and each such council was required
to form from its own numbers a "watch committee" of which the
mayor, *ex officio* a justice of the peace, must be a member. The
watch committee was to provide a twenty-four-hour police force;
it would appoint the men to be sworn in and make regulations for
their governance; it had the power to fire as well as hire.

The Metropolitan Police model clearly had some influence on
this provincial step forward in police administration (and London
police officers were in much demand to assist in helping the new
forces to work), but the act of 1835 did not, by any means, stan-
dardize the forces of the 178 corporate towns (more were char-
tered subsequently) to which it applied. Each watch committee
could impose its own conditions of service: standards of recruitment and rate of pay, numbers engaged—all were at its discretion.
This resulted in widely differing police forces, some built along
good lines, with adequate strength, fit men, and a decent wage;
others perpetuated the bad features of the former regime by simply taking on their old watchmen; others ignored the act; and several were still without regular police fifteen years later.

The government next turned its attention to the rural police,
the police of the counties within which the corporate towns lay.
The County Police Act of 1839 was a hasty attempt to establish
regular police for each of the fifty-six counties of England and
Wales. To prepare the way, the government had appointed a royal
commission, the three members of which were Edwin Chadwick
(who had played a prominent part in the proceedings which led to
the Metropolitan Police Act of 1829), Colonel Rowan, and Shaw
Lefevre (a member of the "squirearchy," rulers of the countryside,
whose traditional preserve was now to be invaded by Parliament).
The commissioners' survey disclosed a sorry state of law-enforcement and order maintenance, with much bias and corruption.
recourse to the military to maintain the peace, and widespread
robbery and burglary with which the existing constables could not
cope. The commissioners recommended adoption of the Metropolitan Police model, with the counties on request being provided
with officers supplied by the Metropolitan Police.

This was too much for the government. Public disorder in the
provinces was about to get out of hand and there was no time to
face opposition from the old order. The act of 1839 therefore con-

fined itself to empowering county magistrates in quarter sessions (which then constituted county government) to establish a police force; the act is known as "the Permissive Act" because the county justices were not obliged to implement it. Though the law did produce a substantial increase in the forces of law and order, only twenty-eight counties set up regular police.

The government had, however, learned that everything should not be left to local discretion—the kind of disparities produced by the Municipal Corporation Act of 1835 were obviously to be avoided—and the home secretary was given power to make regulations for the county police (e.g., as regarded conditions of service and pay), and the appointment of the chief constable of each county force had to have his approval. These powers reserved to the central government were a considerable encroachment on local autonomy and proved a useful model for future police legislation.

The next principal measure was the County and Borough Police Act of 1856, known as "the Obligatory Act." This is the major landmark in the making of Britain's modern police system. The Metropolitan Police Act had produced a model for the conduct of a civil force; the act of 1856 produced a model for the nationwide standardization of police that characterizes the British system today.

The act prescribed that *all* counties were now to establish police forces, for which the home secretary would make regulations, and the chief constables of which had to be approved by him before appointment. The urban centers, the boroughs, nevertheless retained their right to regulate their own forces. However, the home secretary would exercise, through Crown-appointed Inspectors of Constabulary, a certain supervision over both county and urban police services. Statistics of crime were to be compiled by police forces and centralized at the Home Office. Thus, for over 150 years Britain has had a national record of offenses known to the police.

How was this further invasion of local autonomy made acceptable to the existing authorities? The answer is financial. The government undertook to bear a proportion of the cost of such forces as were certified efficient, in terms of numbers and discipline, by the Inspectors of Constabulary. Thus, in 1856, the central and local authorities entered into a partnership for the provision of police services which is still in operation.

The device of inspection of local services by the central government already had been fruitfully employed with respect to factories, prisons, and workhouses, and so it had the British benediction of "precedent." The first Inspectors of Constabulary were all former military officers: Major-General Cartwright, Lieutenant-Colonel Woodford (at the time of appointment Chief Constable of Lancashire), and Captain Willis, a former Chief Constable of Manchester. What the inspectors found out about police efficiency in the early years showed that there was a great deal to be desired. The remedy most urged upon the smaller urban centers, consolidation with the county force, had some good results. From the reports of H.M. Inspectors of Constabulary, published annually from 1857 onwards and presented to parliament, much can be learned about the development of provincial policing (the Metropolitan Police were not subject to their inspection). The power to withhold the government's grant was, of course, a considerable factor in the gradual improvement of the police. The elements of the formula that emerged from the three acts mentioned above were local government's responsibility for maintaining regular police, with a degree of central government aid, supervision and control, the counties being more subject to the central government than the urban centers.

The Local Government Act of 1888 made important changes in the police sphere. Henceforth, no town of less than ten thousand inhabitants was to maintain its own police force: this mandated consolidations. The main thrust of the act was political, putting county government on the same democratic basis as that of the corporate towns. The administrative functions of the quarter sessions of the county justices now would be performed by elected county councils. This raised the question of political control of the county police. Logically, perhaps, this should have been transferred to the county councils but in any case the government decided that county police should be controlled by a special body of a hybrid nature, the Standing Joint Committee, half of the membership of which should be county justices and half members of the county council. This arrangement, anomalous as it may seem (as do so many British institutions), worked very well in practice and survived unaltered until modified by the Police Act of 1964.

As the nineteenth century drew to a close, the criminal statistics bore some witness to the effectiveness of the police in the prevention of crime, the purpose for which those who created the system designed it. Melville Lee* quotes the introduction to *Criminal Statistics for 1898,* which concludes:

> ...that the actual number of crimes brought into the courts had diminished appreciably during the last thirty years; that, if the increase of population is taken into account, the decrease in crime becomes very marked; that, if we also take into account the increase of the police force and the greater efficiency in the means of investigating and punishing crime, we may conclude that the decrease in crime is even greater than the figures show.

Miscellaneous as the police forces were, ranging from the Metropolitan Police of London to the forces of small towns, the nation now had a coherent police system. The ability of civil police to check civil disorder and to contain crime had been amply demonstrated, and the partnership of central government, local government and chief constable was well established.

That Britain did not suffer the revolutionary upheavals of Europe during the century was due to many factors, not the least of which was the presence of the police.

Criminal Investigation

The major police development in the nineteenth century, in the United States as in Britain, was the institution of uniformed civil police, but the same period also saw great progress in systems and techniques of criminal investigation.

The Metropolitan Police had been envisioned in 1829 purely as a uniformed force. No provision was made in the General Instructions for detective duties. There were good reasons for this. In the first place, if the New Police were to be accepted by the public, its style had to be absolutely open. The British nourished a

---

*W.L. Melville Lee, *A History of Police in England,* p. 405.

horror of European policing, especially with regard to its covert activities. Domestic espionage was built into the system of their nearest neighbor, France, and the alarming shade of Fouché, Napoleon's minister of police, together with impressions of the policing of the Ancien Regime, as well as the tales told of police power in Austria and Prussia, had long convinced the islanders that they wanted no part of it. Another reason why the Metropolitan Police was not provided with a detective branch was that there were already detective officers at work in London: the Bow Street Runners and the police at the stipendiary magistrates' courts, that both continued to operate until 1839.

It was not until 1842 that the Metropolitan Police Commissioners formed a small detective unit to work out of their headquarters. Two inspectors and six sergeants, among them a former Bow Street Runner, constituted the staff. We owe to Charles Dickens some lively impressions of the early detectives, whom he entertained in his editorial office at *Household Words,* and Dickens was the first author in English to make a police detective a principal character in a novel. "Inspector Bucket" in *Bleak House* (1852–53) is patently based upon Inspector Charles Frederick Field.

Colonel Sir Charles Rowan had resigned his commissionership in 1850 and it had always been Richard Mayne, the man of law, who had concerned himself with the detectives. They remained under his eye, working as they did from Scotland Yard, for it had been found that when it was a question of fugitive criminals, the Metropolitan Police divisional areas could in their way be as restrictive as the old parish boundaries. The incidence of crime in London, nevertheless, demanded the services of more than the handful of detectives at the Yard, and in 1862 it was ordered that some two hundred divisional officers should be employed in plain clothes. At the time of Mayne's death there were only sixteen detectives in the headquarters unit. They had established a good professional reputation and the practice of provincial police asking for their help in difficult cases had begun.

New criminal problems had appeared in Mayne's later years. The transportation of convicts to Australia had had the effect of permanently removing from Britain nearly all who were so sentenced, but this ceased in 1850, and men who had served their sentences in English prisons returned to a society that wanted nothing to do with them. Many took to street crime, and a form of robbery with violence called "garrotting"—half strangling the victim— became rife.

Political terrorism struck in 1867, the work of the American-based Fenian movement, which had made Home Rule for Ireland its aim. An explosion wrecked a street of houses in Clerkenwell, killing four people and injuring forty. The perpetrators were caught, but the detectives henceforth had to tackle a new kind of criminal—the political fanatic. The Yard men had to cast their net wide and make many journeys to the provincial centers particularly associated with the Fenians, notably Liverpool and Manchester. Fenian terrorism in 1883, in the form of the dynamiting of public buildings, caused the authorities at Scotland Yard to form the Special Irish Branch (now the Special Branch) to operate against the dynamiters, who were duly suppressed. Most of the staff of the Special Irish Branch were Irish. In the following century the first professional policeman to receive the honor of knighthood was a head of the Special Branch, Patrick Quinn.

Mayne was succeeded in 1869 (he had died, still in office, the previous year) by Colonel Edmund Henderson, formerly of the Royal Engineers, who had spent the last thirteen years of his life administering convicts in Australia and serving as Surveyor-General of Prisons at the Home Office in London. His interest in crime led him to make immediate changes in the detective organization. The expedient of putting some officers in each division into plain clothes had not worked at all well. Henderson decreed that there should be a detective unit of ten men in each division and that the central unit should be increased to over forty. It was intended that the divisional detectives should deal with routine criminal work and that the Yard men would come in on difficult or specialized cases. The latter also made inquiries, at the instigation of the government, into such matters as extradition and the activities of aliens.

The divisional arrangements looked well enough on paper, but in practice they proved unsatisfactory. Detectives cannot be created by a stroke of the pen. Although Henderson had ordered that the divisional detectives should be "selected from the most promising men in the service" and given enhanced pay, the en-

hancement was minimal, and the divisional superintendents were
not putting their best officers into detective work. There was poor
liaison among the different groups of divisional detectives, and
manpower was used wastefully in order to save money (a perennial complaint against police administration). Altogether, the system
was unproductive and a grave crisis in the detective department at
Scotland Yard brought this to light.

Since 1874 a group of race track swindlers had been operating
with singular impunity. Whenever an attempt was made to arrest
them, they had always just moved on. It became clear that someone at Scotland Yard was keeping them informed of the investigation into their affairs. The authorities were alarmed, and with good
reason, for when the matter was sifted it was found necessary to
prosecute three of the five most senior officers of the detective
branch for conspiracy to defeat the ends of justice. Two were
found guilty and sentenced to imprisonment; the third retired immediately after the trial. The case was widely reported and public
confidence in Scotland Yard was shaken badly.

The state of affairs which would lead to "the trial of the detectives" in 1877 caused the home secretary, earlier in that year, to
appoint a departmental commission to inquire into "the state, discipline and organization of the Detective Force of the Metropolitan Police."

The members of the commission took a great deal of evidence,
from such a variety of witnesses and sources that their report almost constitutes a comparative study of criminal police administration—Metropolitan Police officers and officials, provincial and
Scottish police chiefs, a superintendent from Dublin; letters were
sent to the United States, Austria, and France.

Some of the testimony is eloquent regarding police attitudes
toward detective duty; before the force was half a century old,
modern professional dogma was already established. The consensus of police evidence held by Sir Richard Mayne, who "would
not allow anyone to join the detective service unless he joined in
the usual way as a uniform constable." The vocation for detective
work was acknowledged, in homely and unromantic terms, as
when a divisional superintendent was questioned:

> The promotion in the detective branch is of course not great?
>> It is not.
> If they want promotion they have to leave it?

Yes; but they seldom do ... There is still a great liking for the detective business; they are in plain clothes; they have more discretion; and they are in some cases exposed to less danger. They are also better protected from the weather.

A detective sergeant was pressed on the value of education to a detective. He said,

I do not think a man of education catches more thieves than a man without education.

You do not think that, as long as you get shrewdness and intelligence ... education really assists you?

I do not think that it does, as far as I have seen. I have not seen those men catching thieves so well as the others, so long as I have been in the police. I think you will find that it is not the men of first-rate education who have caught thieves.

The statistics foreshadowed some recent American research when they revealed that, out of 82 cases of burglary, only 1 arrest was made by a divisional detective, and in the 249 serious offenses against property recorded in one month of 1877 in the Metropolitan Police District, only 28 arrests were made. Of these, 9 were made on the spot by uniform officers or private persons; three by divisional detectives; 10 by uniform officers and divisional detectives conjointly; the remaining 6 by uniform officers on their own. The figures for the full year showed a total arrest rate by all detectives (headquarters and divisional) of 23.8 percent. The superintendent from the Dublin Metropolitan Police probably caused a sensation when he announced that "their" arrest rate, as far as his own divisional detectives were concerned, was 80 to 85 percent.

None of this professional evidence, however, was as influential as a paper submitted by a gentlemen of twenty-eight years of age, who had never been in the police service at all. Howard Vincent was a former army officer, a great traveller and linguist, a newspaper foreign correspondent and a tyro lawyer with a year's unremunerative practice at the Bar. He had taken the initiative, when he learned of the inquiry, to make a visit on his own to Paris, in order to study the detective organization at the Prefecture of Police, whose work in criminal investigation was generally regarded as the best in the world. What impressed Vincent most seems to have been the centralization of the French detective department.

The members of the commission recommended "the establishment of a united and distinct force for that particular branch of police work," that "the men composing it should, in their respective ranks, take precedence of the uniform or preventive branch of the service," and that the detective force should be placed under a lawyer with experience as a magistrate.

The home secretary did not appoint a lawyer with magisterial experience. He appointed Howard Vincent, with the title of Director of Criminal Investigations, and the rank of assistant commissioner.

As recommended, the detective department was reorganized along unitary lines under the name it still bears, the Criminal Investigation Department. The effect of the reorganization of 1878 was to make the CID "a force within a force," a jealously guarded enclave in the midst of the Metropolitan Police. The CID, not the divisional superintendents, would now select entrants from the uniform branch, whether for employment at Scotland Yard or with one of the divisions; a move from the CID back to uniform would be thought of as a kind of demotion. On the one hand the department would eventually build great, unique and acclaimed expertise; on the other, its new constitution engendered a split between detective and uniform officers, with the detectives' loyalty going first to the CID and secondly to the force. The solidarity of the detectives became a byword and its inbred nature would favor some unhappy developments in time to come. The department brought into operation under Howard Vincent, nevertheless, would survive with little alteration for almost a hundred years.

The later nineteenth century saw the application of the physical sciences to police work. Alphonse Bertillon (1853–1934) made a very great contribution as the pioneer of scientific identification. He invented a system, "anthropometry," to identify recidivists, hitherto a chancy affair relying on eyewitness testimony. He was also a pioneer in the techniques connected with the scene of crime, in police photography (it was Bertillon who devised the *portrait parlé*, "the speaking likeness"—the methodical description of a photograph, still a standard component of police identification systems), and in other criminalistic matters. His work at the Prefecture of Police of Paris was rapidly recognized by the world's police forces and it was adopted in New York, Chicago, and London soon after its discovery.

The anthropometric system was time consuming and it was hard to attain a uniform precision in measurement taking. Another system of identification was soon largely to supersede it, this time of British provenance.

In 1880 a letter appeared in the journal *Nature,* written by Henry Faulds (1843–1930), a Scottish medical missionary working in Tokyo. Faulds had studied the skin patterns of the fingertips and convinced himself of their permanence, and he had even identified a thief by comparing his fingerprints with prints left at the scene of the crime. His letter propounded the view that fingerprints could lead to the scientific identification of criminals. Meanwhile, in India, a senior British administrator, William Herschel (1833–1917), had long been at work establishing the permanence of fingerprints and exploring their individuality; he was satisfied that a person could be identified by fingerprints.

Dr. Faulds's letter in *Nature* spurred Herschel to reply and publicize his own work. The subject attracted official attention; Herschel's work received more notice than Faulds's. Francis Galton (1822–1911), the leading general scientist in Britain, confirmed by long research the permanence and individuality of fingerprints. In India, another British administrator, Edward Henry (1850–1931), studied the subject, came home to see Galton, and with Galton's help devoted himself to the problem, left largely unsolved by Galton, of how to classify and file the prints. In this he had excellent assistance from Indian police officers under his command as Inspector-General of Police in Lower Bengal. Henry solved the problem by a classification of types of patterns and numbers of ridges in a person's prints. This system proved readily adaptable for police use, as demonstrated by its successful use in Bengal, and Scotland Yard adopted it in 1901. Henry came with the system, being appointed assistant commissioner and head of the Criminal Investigation Department.

Tremendous credit is obviously due to all the men mentioned above, but whether the primacy should be given to Faulds or to Herschel has been in dispute for nearly a century. Professor John J. Cronin, after a recent survey of the subject, offers a reasoned view: "It would seem that a fair appraisal of relative credit would be arrived at by conceding Herschel's priority in the conception which would prevent crime through registration of fingerprints, whereas Faulds had the earlier inspiration of the use of chance prints for the detection of criminals."*

Other nineteenth-century pioneers in scientific criminal investigation should be mentioned. Dr. Hans Gross (1847–1915), an Austrian criminal magistrate, wrote a key book on the subject, first published in 1893, that became known in an English version in 1906—translated and "adapted," and adapted again and again by successive editors. No evidence has come to light that Arthur Conan Doyle ever met Gross, though Gross, most catholic of criminalists, recommended the Sherlock Holmes stories for serious reading; there are some odd similarities in the case studies of the Irish storyteller and the Austrian judge. Neither can be ignored in the transformation of detective procedure which took place at the end of the century.

That century saw the by no means untroubled evolution of detective organization in London, where the investigators became a distinct and privileged order of police, and Scotland Yard's became, *par excellence,* the preeminent detective department. Since 1871, the Metropolitan Police had been required by law to maintain records of persons found guilty of crime in England and Wales. The services of the Criminal Record Office then set up were available to all police forces in the country. In the following century the national fingerprint collection would be housed similarly at New Scotland Yard. These facilities contributed greatly to the primacy London's police enjoyed among their provincial peers.

In the provinces detective work was done under different conditions. The county police forces, thinly spread, with many a "village policeman" on his own, and the small police forces of most urban centers, rarely made the sharp distinction between the detective and preventive operations of their service. There was far more interchange between plain clothes and uniform, far less mystique, and little or no question of "departmental," as opposed to "force," allegiance.

---

*"The Fingerprinters," in Philip John Stead's *Pioneers in Policing,* p. 166.

Policing in the Nineteenth Century

It is not to be imagined that the instituting of regular police forces wrought miracles in bringing tranquility and decorum to nineteenth-century Britain. Though the roaring violence of the earlier part of the century abated in the later part, as the great displacement of the Industrial Revolution settled down and the new urban populations habituated themselves to city living, Victorian society always had contradictions: a stolid respectability and a voracious appetite for pleasure; a movement by successive consensus to greater democracy and a deep-rooted discontent with the extent of its progress.

The cities, despite their police, still had their criminal neighborhoods; street prostitution was flagrant; the countryside was plagued with vagrants. Public disorders on a large scale recurred, elections all over the country giving rise to partisan strife, and political causes generating violent protest. Sir Richard Mayne, nearing the end of his four-decade commissionership, was injured in the Hyde Park Riots (over parliamentary reform) in 1866. Cavanagh recalls him, sitting his horse, commanding at the scene: "The poor old fellow, sticking to his post in the most gallant manner, and giving orders right and left, was struck in the face by some cowardly scoundrels by stones thrown at him, the blood streaming down his venerable face."[*]

It must have been heartbreaking for Mayne, so late in his great career, to have to call in the military to support the overmatched police in restoring order, the first time since 1829. The London mob, the destructive element which tagged on to any demonstration that could be turned into mischief, was still there, as it was everywhere. A series of violent confrontations provoked by radicals took place in 1887, culminating in a mass march at which the police cordons succeeded in preventing the occupation by the demonstrators of Trafalgar Square, but again the military had to be brought in, at the commissioner's request, to give necessary support.

On these and many other less spectacular occasions the police-

[*]T.A. Cavanagh, *Scotland Yard Past and Present*, pp. 79–80.

man's life was at risk. Frederick Porter Wensley, who eventually became London's senior detective, joined the Metropolitan Police in 1887, whereupon he received a few weeks' drill and was sent out on a beat to learn his business by himself. He learned it the hard way, in *L* Division, in Lambeth, and a harder way still when he was transferred four years later to Whitechapel. Any complacency over the civilizing of Victorian London is dispelled as Wensley records: "Gangs of hooligans infested the streets and levied blackmail on timorous shopkeepers. There was an enormous amount of personal robbery with violence. The maze of narrow ill lighted alleys offered easy ways of escape after a man had been knocked down and his watch and money stolen."* It was in that maze that Jack the Ripper had vanished in 1888.

Adversity indeed characterized police work during its first regular century. Discipline was harsh, police authorities often capricious. In London, Mayne never relaxed the draconian severity of the force's first years; once he fired about sixty men reported for being drunk on duty at Christmas. Uniform had to be worn off duty as well as on, subjecting each officer to a continuous visibility by a public always ready to denounce his slightest shortcomings. The pay was small for the hours of work demanded, and pension prospects uncertain. It was not until 1890 that all police were given a statutory right to pension; until then, pensions were "granted" (or not) on various terms by the Home Office to Metropolitan Police officers or the police authorities of the counties and urban centers.

Vacations were equally variable feasts. The sergeants and constables of the county of Hampshire were "no doubt all grateful when in 1875 the number of days leave in the year was increased from four to seven."† It was usual for a police officer to be on duty each day (or night) for several weeks on end, working his beat in all weathers. The damage to health was heavy and the high rate of wastage of manpower that prevailed during the period was to a considerable extent due to sickness. It was not until 1910 that Parliament enacted a weekly rest day for the police. Leave and other

*Frederick Porter Wensley, *Detective Days,* p. 8.
†Ian A. Watt, *A History of the Hampshire & Isle of Wight Constabulary, 1839–1966,* p. 29.

conditions of service were regulated by the police authorities, central or local, without consultation with the great body of the service. This became a bitter, ingrained grievance, the fact that the police had no "right to confer" with their employers.

In 1872 there was a small strike in London on this issue, grimly repressed by the authorities; in 1890 there was a more serious strike on the same question: this time, the military had to be called in to restore order. Thirty-nine constables were fired and never reinstated.

The right to vote in parliamentary and municipal elections was denied to police officers until 1887 and 1893 respectively, in which years Police Disabilities Removal Acts became law.*

Adverse conditions are not always negative in their effects. Military and police forces with the toughest induction training, universities and schools with the most stringent entrance examinations, never lack applicants. The hard and dangerous work of the police, with its incessant demands and harsh discipline, most certainly forged a bond among those who could stand up to it, and gave police a corporate morale of sterling quality. Otherwise, the history of the British police would have been very different.

British Police Models in a Wider World

Regular policing was developed in Ireland well ahead of the regular forces that appeared in England from 1829 onwards. Pitt's abortive police bill of 1785 became the Dublin Police Act of 1786, whereby three justices were appointed as commissioners and the city was divided into four police areas, each with a chief constable and ten petty constables, over whom was a high constable, who was under the commissioners. In its early years unpopular and apparently inefficient, the Dublin police was nevertheless to have a long life, taking its final form from an act of 1836 that matched the system with that of the Metropolitan Police of London, the home secretary's role being taken by the Lord Lieutenant of Ireland. The force was consolidated in 1925 with the *Gárdá Síochána*, the police of the new republic.

*T.A. Critchley, *A History of Police in England and Wales*, p. 166.

Robert Peel, as mentioned in Chapter 3, had formed in 1814 a civil police, to be established wherever disturbances occurred, but it was the force created by the Constabulary (Ireland) Act of 1836 which was to be the model for police development in several parts of the world. The Irish Constabulary (Royal Irish Constabulary, from 1867) widely differed from the police forces of Great Britain. Its style was military, with dark green uniforms; arms were routinely carried; there was direct entrance to supervisory and command levels, creating an "officer" and "other rank" division, just what Peel had been resolute in avoiding in London. The men lived in barracks, isolating them from the community; from the outset there were training centers along soldierly lines for the induction of recruits. But the grand difference lay in the control: here it was vested in the central government in Dublin Castle, whereas in England all police except the Metropolitan were under local authorities.

It is tempting to categorize the Royal Irish Constabulary as a *gendarmerie,* but this is to misrepresent the character of the force. The RIC were not soldiers, as gendarmes are soldiers: gendarmes receive full military training and are part of the regular army, liable to be called upon for combatant service in war. The men of the RIC were not privates, but constables, and their military mien went with an essentially civil status.

The Royal Irish Constabulary was disbanded in 1922, when the Civic Guard was formed to police the twenty-six counties of the Irish Free State, but its tradition was continued in the formation of the Royal Ulster Constabulary for the six counties of Northern Ireland.

The development of the Indian Police Service was directly influenced by General Sir Charles Napier's adaptation of the Royal Irish Constabulary model, when he was responsible for the administration of the large and crime-ridden province of Scind, immediately after his conquest and annexation of that country. In 1843 Napier formed a police, under British officers, entirely separate from the army and with none but police duties. This proved so effective in the repression of crime that it was copied some ten years later in Bombay and Madras, and when the Indian Police Commission was appointed in 1860 with the task of surveying the existing police system and recommending improvements, the government of India's memorandum to the commissioners reflected its acceptance of the kind of policing which Napier had introduced.

The Police Act of 1861, based on the commission's report, may be said to constitute the charter of the Indian Police Service. It provided for a civil police force to be formed in each province of the subcontinent, controlled by an inspector-general responsible to the provincial government; the force would have none but police duties and would be recruited, trained, disciplined, commanded, and administered by British officers. The act gave this vast country, with its great variety of peoples, languages, and cultures, a uniform police system for the first time in its tumultuous history. The association with the Royal Irish Constabulary continued, as many of the latter's officers joined the Indian Police. The other ranks, up to sub-inspector, were Indian, but from 1912 onwards sincere efforts were made to fill a proportion of the higher ranks with suitably qualified Indians. By the time of Independence in 1947, almost one-third of them were so staffed.

The Indian Police, though never numerous in relation to India's enormous population—the total strength in 1901 was 163,116*—quickly achieved a remarkable level of efficiency. Its creation of specialist branches to deal with specific types of crime, notably dacoity, the widespread and alarmingly professional robbery committed by groups of men whose families had often been active in this sphere for generations, antedated this recourse in Britain and America. The legendary criminal intelligence system, associated with what was until the Second World War Britain's major intelligence operation (of which Rudyard Kipling wrote so memorably in 1901 in *Kim*), was highly developed; it was in India that fingerprinting first became a practical police technique. Sir Percival Griffiths, a former magistrate and administrator in India, reviewed the Indian Police's record at the moment of Independence:

> Much indeed had been achieved in ninety years. Thuggee and the cult of poisoning were things of the past; dacoity had been brought under control; scientific technique had been applied to the detection of crime; and life had been made secure for the ordinary citizen. A

*Sir Percival Griffiths, *To Guard My People,* p. 423.

man could send his wife or children from one end of the country to the other in safety, and a merchant could remit funds knowing that they would reach their destination.

This indeed is what the British Empire in India had meant, and one of its main instruments had been the Indian police system. In these developments a leading role had been played by the officers of that great service, the Indian police: Many and diverse were the gifts which they brought to their task. Some had a flair for the detection of crime; others were born organizers of men; and nearly all had moral and physical courage of a high order. More important even than these qualities was the capacity for leadership which so many of them possessed. By virtue of this quality they welded men of many races and creeds into an effective force, and they bequeathed to independent India a reliable instrument for the maintenance of law and order.[*]

As the Royal Irish Constabulary had done, the Indian Police proved a model for other forces: in Burma, Malaya, East Africa, and in the colonial empire at large. The two models, Irish and Indian, each created in times of great turbulence, offered a simple, workable kind of organization, featuring central direction, military style, strong command and supervision, and close cadres. The colonial forces were unitary, one for each country, like the RIC, while the Indian Police was, as it were, ninefold, with one force in each of India's nine provinces.

The "home" police model of Britain, based in style though not in structure on the London Metropolitan Police, also found its way overseas. If Canada developed a police brilliantly adapted to the needs of a huge country and a new state, the states of Australia adopted, or rather, adapted, the home model to the needs of a much larger country. New Zealand in 1886, formed a national civil police, unarmed, with a minister of police taking the role of the home secretary in his relationship with the Metropolitan Police.

Whether or not any model influenced its instigators, chief of whom was Canada's first prime minister, Sir John A. Macdonald, the Northwest Mounted Police proved marvellously apt for its herculean task. Founded in 1873 to police the prairies, where

*Sir Percival Griffiths, ibid., pp. 412–13.

whiskey and firearms were being traded to the Indians, and where the tide of settlers from the east threatened to bring with it the kind of conflict which occurred in the United States, the force was armed and uniformed. Its first commissioner, Lieutenant Colonel George A. French, commanded it in a way that could be only semimilitary, so much of the work having to be done individually by the constables on their own initiative.

Responsibilities increased with the nation's growth; the force found itself patrolling the border, collecting customs dues, repressing rebellion, caring for the health and welfare of Indians and Eskimos, and policing the Klondike gold rush of 1896, while carrying on its patrol of the vast plains of western and central Canada.

Other police organizations sprang up at this time. Towns, cities and counties began to replace old ways of watch keeping with regular police forces, however small. In 1867 came the creation of the provinces of Canada, individually responsible for the adminstration of justice: this led to the formation of provincial police which, like the state police of the United States, varied widely in size and function.

To the Northwest Mounted Police, however, must go the credit for having forestalled the chaos and bloodshed that unpoliced settlement would inevitably have produced. They were there at the outset, developing empirically to do what had to be done, and their success in doing it made them one of the world's most respected and admired police forces.

Dutch and British custom had dictated the police arrangements of the colonial era in America, and the old order survived the revolution for several decades. New York in 1800 had a high constable, sixteen constables and seventy-two watchmen, plus forty marshals (mayor appointed and paid by results), and it was not until the 1840s and 1850s that the great cities of the east initiated regular police on a twenty-four-hour basis. During the great drive westward, from 1848 the ancient institutions of the sheriff and the *posse comitatus* took a new lease of life; as the West settled down towards the end of the century, the modern pattern of county sheriffs' departments and municipal police emerged. Only Texas, and to a much lesser degree Massachusetts, formed state police agencies during this period. Federal policing, however, was established in the form of United States Marshals (since 1789), Postal Inspectors (1829), the Secret Service (1865), and the Customs Border Patrol (1886), but these agencies had few personnel; the local tradition of police sank deeper roots in American administration. While Britain strove to reduce the number of local police forces and the central government entered increasingly into the regulation of police affairs, in the United States a robust determination to keep local matters in local hands resulted in a grand proliferation of police agencies, reflecting the reinvigoration, for good and ill, of a tradition which in Britain was already much eroded.

CHAPTER 6

The Police Before the Second World War

Command and Control

By 1900, the British police were nearing the end of their first great phase of professional development. The fundamental skills in prevention, detection, and proof of crime, and the maintenance of public tranquility, had been demonstrated, and above all, the police had won the acceptance of the great majority of citizens. This last achievement was due to the "presence" the police had established in urban and rural communities, a presence that militated against transgressors of the laws, but that also made available at all hours, day and night, a service to which people could appeal in emergencies great and small, imparting a new sense of security.

Professional skills, indeed, but no one regarded the police officer as a professional man. Peel's distinction persisted: the policeman, even in the dignity of plain clothes, was not considered to be of officer status in anything like the same sense as a second lieutenant in the army. The clearest indication of this distinction was to be seen in the appointment of police chiefs.

Commissioners of Police of the Metropolis were appointed

from outside the service, just as Rowan and Mayne, of necessity, had been. Not until 1959 would anyone who had joined the force as a constable be made commissioner. Before then, of the fifteen who had held office since 1829, ten had been officers of the armed services (several indeed had held nonmilitary posts also, of an administrative nature), three came from Indian Police posts, one (Mayne) was a lawyer, and one a senior civil servant. The assistant commissioners, too, had similarly recognized "professional" backgrounds. In the larger counties, military officers predominated among the chief constables; in the cities and boroughs, although those who rose from the ranks had a better chance of reaching the top posts, again the military were well represented. It was felt in the circles where the most important chief officer appointments were made that experience in commissioned ranks, or comparable experience elsewhere, was needed to command the police.

In practice, this feeling was not without advantages. In the social climate then prevailing, it was no bad thing for the police chief to be regarded as on equal terms with the people constituting the police authority. With a foot in both worlds, he was likelier to be able to speak up for his force and be an intermediary between the police and the public, someone to be counted on not to take merely a "police" view of the relationship. Centuries of nonprofessional peace keeping and law enforcement lay behind all this: the magistrates and constables of the old dispensation, were in office only because they had status in the community in other capacities, whether as landlords or householders. Nor can it be said that the rank and file of the service were wholly opposed to the outsiders: old habits of respect for the gentry died hard, and when it came to discipline, many a policeman preferred to be judged by someone other than people like himself.

Obsolescent as such a state of affairs may seem today it had a lot of vitality. The great police pioneers were all outsiders, and in the present century there have been many outstanding chiefs who did not come up from the ranks. As late as 1929, a Royal Commission on Police Powers and Procedures reported:

> ...Long experience and good service in the lower ranks of the Force are not the only, or even the most important, qualifications for the higher posts, which ought to be filled by men who, besides being .

themselves upright and fair-minded, are capable of impressing their own standards on their subordinates. We should therefore regard as inimical to the public interest any system which limited appointments to the higher posts to those who had entered the police as constables and we are of opinion that such posts should be filled by the best men available, irrespective of the source whence they are drawn.

Thus in 1902, for instance, the Liverpool Watch Committee appointed their deputy chief, Mr. Leonard (later Sir Leonard) Dunning, educated at Eton and Oxford, with several years commissioned service in the Royal Irish Constabulary as their chief constable. Dunning proved an exceptionally effective chief there for ten years, whereupon he was appointed one of H.M. Inspectors of Constabulary. His annual reports reflect his concern for the good management of the service, as when he wrote in 1919.*

In the organisation of a police force one must not stand still, the two processes of centralisation and decentralisation must be continually applied to each detail of police work, with a view to securing uniformity of action in circumstances which can be anticipated and defined by instruction, along with intelligence and boldness of individual action in circumstances novel and unpredicted.

The axioms by which the application of the opposing processes must be guided may be stated:

Decentralise as far as you can, centralize as far as you must.

Decentralise for action, centralise for instruction, criticism and record.

It is interesting to note that Raymond B. Fosdick, some six years earlier,* wrote that "Decentralise as far as you can; centralise as far as you must" was "the maxim of Scotland Yard, its program of organization."

The nineteenth century had seen strong and salient initiatives in the police sphere on the part of the central government. The creation of the Metropolitan Police under direct central control; the bringing into being of municipal police forces in 1835, and

*This was communicated to the author by the late F.T. Tarry, C.B., C.B.E, M.M., K.P.M., formerly one of H.M. Inspectors, who thought that Sir Leonard might have brought this doctrine over from the Royal Irish Constabulary.

†Raymond B. Fosdick, *European Police Systems,* p. 107.

county police in 1839 and 1856; the institution of the Inspectorate of Constabulary in 1856: these were measures in which the
government had to come to terms with the old order of en-
trenched local independence. Thus, although the home secretary
controlled the Metropolitan Police, the municipal government
had a firm grip on the urban police; and the county police, though
subject to a greater degree of central control, were substantially
under their local authority, the standing joint committee, which
had taken over this function from the old quarter sessions.

No radical change in the political control of the police took
place in the twentieth century before the Second World War, except for some futher incursions by the central government into
local police affairs under the Police Act of 1919. The Metropolitan
Police continued to be under the control of the home secretary (as
they still are), operating under Peel's Act of 1829. While there had
been conflict between a commissioner (General Sir Charles War-
ren) and the home secretary of the day over their respective
spheres of authority over the force, culminating in the commissioner's resignation in 1888, the relationship was normally one
that left command to the commissioner, with the minister having
ultimate control and answering to Parliament for his conduct of
the force.

In the urban centers, the watch committee of the municipal
council ("a sufficient number, not exceeding one-third of its own
body") was very much in control, although the Inspector of Constabulary's certificate of efficiency in the force's numbers and discipline was necessary for the committee to secure the central government's grant (since 1874 this amounted to one-half of the cost
of the force's pay and clothing), the watch committee made its own
regulations concerning remuneration and conditions of service;
appointed and dismissed the chief constable; made all promotions;
and acted as the disciplinary authority. The extent to which a chief
constable was able to influence rewards and punishments within
his force thus depended upon his relationship with the watch committee. It needs little imagination to visualize how many kinds of
situations this discretionary state of affairs could produce, and how
political influence and patronage could impair the effectiveness
and impartiality of the police, the authority of the chief officer, and
the morale of the men. The main check on the watch committee

was that it had to submit matters of expenditure to the vote of the whole municipal council, another factor of uncertainty, another channel for interference. The quality of urban police forces varied widely throughout the country, according to the policies of committees and councils as well as the character and capacity of chief constables.

The county police forces were administered very differently. The standing joint committee, half the members of which were justices and half councilors, while subject to the home secretary's approval of appointments and dismissals of chief officers, and the numbers and pay of the force, was very much more independent of the county council, notably in that its expenditure (as approved by the home secretary) had to be met by the council. The county chief constable was also very much more independent than his municipal counterpart, having the power to appoint, promote, discipline, and dismiss his officers. The hapless municipal chief often had to see his men buttonholing the members of the watch committee or appealing to them against his decisions.*

A Crisis of Morale

Legislation in 1867 and 1884 gave the working class entry to political power: they could now vote and exert influence in Parliament. In 1893 the Labour party was formed, with aims very different from those of the two major parties, the Conservative and the Liberal—aims that were based on tenets of social and economic equality. And although the Labour party did not achieve a firm grasp of government until the end of the Second World War, its platform and alliance with the trade unions, which contributed most of its funds, made it a political force of rapidly growing magnitude. The policeman's aspiration to a "right to confer" with his employers must be seen in the context of the new political stature of the class to which nearly all policemen belonged.

Militancy in the quest for representation emerged unmistak-

---

*The novels of Maurice Procter, himself a former police officer, such as *No Proud Chivalry* (1947), present a graphic and rather somber picture of what life was like in a medium-sized municipal police force during the years just before the Second World War.

ably in 1913 when the National Union of Police and Prison Officers was formed. Its first secretary, ex-Inspector John Syme, had no reason to love the management of the police service. An educated man of stern principles, he had been too cavalierly treated by the Metropolitan Police hierarchy. He was dismissed from the force in 1910; in 1911, he made threats against home secretary Winston Churchill and was sentenced to six months' imprisonment. His inflamed sense of grievance made him erratic. He was replaced as secretary of the union in 1917; 1924 found him detained as a criminal lunatic. In 1931 the government awarded him compensation for his original mistreatment by the Metropolitan Police. It is significant that a man who had suffered injustice from the authorities should have played a key part in the fight for representation, for what was to come was the result of abysmal mismanagement of police affairs.

The formation of the union was regarded with hostility by the authorities. There was fear that the Trades Union Congress had designs on the control of the police, and it was reasoned that a unionized police would be incapable of impartiality in coping with industrial strife. In London, Commissioner Sir Edward Henry published an order forbidding any officer to join the union under penalty of dismissal. The union, nevertheless, went on recruiting nationwide, and took care to keep its membership records secret—it was a recruitment effort by a Metropolitan Police constable that, when brought to the commissioner's notice, would result in his dismissal and provide a pretext for a strike.

During the First World War the additional burdens the police had to bear were aggravated by the wretched pay that they were receiving: it was barely at subsistence level, less than an agricultural laborer's; teen-age girls in munitions factories were getting three times as much as a constable on overtime with a wife and family to keep. The authorities were aware of this perilous position; Sir Edward Henry was pressing for pay raises for his men, but the home secretary and his bureaucracy were reluctant to move. They were on the verge of acting to increase police pay when events overtook them.

The unrest in the Metropolitan Police, solidly based on the feeling that the authorities were not being fair to them, as well as their very real financial distress, had grown to an extent unappreciated by the administration. The force was commanded and supervised by people mostly past their prime. The commissioner, who wanted to retire before the war, had stayed on at the government's request to see the force over the period of hostilities—he was sixty-eight in 1918; many divisional superintendents had likewise remained in office. Thousands of experienced officers had gone into the armed services. Four years of the stress and drain of the terrible struggle in France had well-nigh exhausted those who had to keep things going in Britain. The war was nearing its end in 1918, but no one knew it, and the seizure of power in Russia by the Bolsheviks in the previous October had led governments everywhere to dread a similar disaster for themselves.

August 1918 found the National Union of Police and Prison Officers ready to attack.

The dismissal of Constable Tommy Thiel for his clandestine recruiting activities on August 25th gave the union a martyr and a pretext for an ultimatum to the commissioner: they demanded a pay increase, reinstatement of Thiel, and recognition of the union. This was delivered on August 27th, with a deadline of compliance at midnight on August 28th. Sir Edward Henry was on leave in Ireland, and it was the acting commissioner who took the ultimatum to the Home Office, where both the home secretary and his senior civil servant were also absent on leave. It was decided to make no reply to the union. The bureaucrats and the police hierarchs down to and including divisional superintendents were convinced that the force would not refuse duty.

They were wrong. The union's preparations had been thorough. On August 29th the headquarters of each division began to report the nonappearance of the night relief. By midnight, August 30th, almost the whole of London's police had struck.

The prime minister himself, David Lloyd George, turned his attention from the war to the home front. At this juncture, with few troops available and only hastily brought in special constables to perform the essential uniform duties, and with revolution in the air, Lloyd George was not the man to leave the police crisis to a home secretary and a commissioner who had so badly misjudged the situation. He solved the problem with characteristic trenchancy and guile.

A substantial pay rise was granted. Thiel could be reinstated.

And recognition of the union? Lloyd George said that he did not think it would be appropriate in wartime. The delegates left him well satisfied that once the war was over, the union would be recognized. The police returned to duty. There was no witch-hunt. A scapegoat was at hand, however: Sir Edward Henry left immediately.

Reform

Further trouble from the union's militants could be confidently expected and the government installed a soldier to succeed Henry. Lieutenant General Sir Nevil Macready was no stranger to trouble in the police sphere; he had been called in for public order emergencies before the war. Moreover, he had the qualities of character and intellect that the present situation demanded. His incisive commissionership bridged the difficult period of readjustment after the strike.

The government, now uncomfortably aware that the state of the police throughout the country left much to be desired, appointed a committee under a senior judge, Lord Desborough, to examine police pay and conditions of service. The committee wasted no time, rapidly concluding that the pay was insufficient, and recommended a substantial raise. The government agreed and granted the increase. Legislation also was begun to set up representative machinery whereby the "right to confer" could be given without unionizing the police.

The union militants, seeing power escaping from them, despite the fact that the police by and large were content with the pay raise, on July 29, 1919 called a second strike. In London it was ineffective; barely a thousand officers refused duty—General Macready's tactics were sound—but in the provinces there was a significant response to the call; notably in Liverpool, where the police force was badly administered. In this city, where religious strife and riot were always to be feared, full advantage was taken of the opportunity for mischief that the withdrawal of half the police presented. What ensued was a mob riot, looting and destruction, during which whole districts were wrecked, and the army had to be sent in to help the remaining regular police and special constables restore order.

All who obeyed the second strike call, some two thousand men throughout the country, were dismissed, never to be reinstated. The National Union of Police and Prison Officers was dead, killed by the pay raise and the promise of representative machinery, a promise that would be kept by the founding of the Police Federation of England and Wales.

The Desborough Committee's recommendations, rapidly submitted, were as rapidly translated into legislation. The Police Act of 1919 provided for the establishment of a Police Council on which all concerned in police administration should be represented—the home secretary, the police authorities of counties and urban centers, and all ranks of the police service from commissioners and chiefs to constables—so that administrative measures could be discussed by those affected prior to implementation. The council's function was to advise; it could not mandate. This was a great step forward in the governance of the police, i.e., recognition that the service, miscellaneous as it was, had common concerns. From 1919 no force was an island, whether it wanted to be one or not: the act provided for the standardization of pay and conditions of service for the whole country. The municipal councils thus lost some of their former autonomy. The variations among cities and counties would now be leveled by the home secretary after consultation with the Police Council. The grant from central taxes towards the maintenance of local police was, at the same time, made more substantial; henceforth, it would amount to one-half of the total cost of the force, not half the cost of pay and uniforms as before.

The Police Federation, designed to represent all members of the service under the rank of superintendent, was established on the basis on which it still stands. In each force there were to be three branch boards, one each for the inspector, sergeant, and constable ranks. An annual conference would be held, at which all forces would be represented; at this conference, central committees for each of the three ranks would be elected and these combined constituted the Joint Central Committee that would speak for it to the home secretary and before the Police Council. The act stipulated that questions of discipline and, except on general principles, promotion were outside the federation's scope. It stated that the federation was intended to enable members of the police to bring to the notice of police authorities and the home secretary "all matters affecting their welfare and efficiency." It was forbidden for a police officer to join a trade union, and it became a criminal offense to induce a police officer to go on strike.

Many would be the troubles of the young federation in attaining its proper place in the world of police administration. Its historian, Anthony Judge, has written of the early years:*

> ... Many chief constables regarded the Federation as an unnecessary appendage to their establishment, decreed by well-meaning fools in the Home Office. Chief officers of the time fell into two main categories: well-bred Army officers who had found secure billets in a civilian, but still uniformed, service, and long service policemen who had climbed every rung of the ladder during many years of harsh discipline. Few of them made any effort to encourage the new branch boards. They regarded welfare as their own province, and it was to be many years before Desborough's second definition of the Federation's work, efficiency, became accepted as a legitimate interest for the federated ranks.

Among the benefits brought by the act was one greatly prized and stoutly defended by police officers ever since: entitlement to free living accommodations, or an allowance in lieu thereof. The act states: "Every member of a police force shall either be provided with a house or quarters free of rent, rates (i.e., local taxes) and taxes (i.e., national taxes), or shall be granted a non-pensionable allowance in lieu."

With the passing into law of the Desborough Committee's far-sighted and realistic recommendations, the British police entered the second great phase of their professionalization. The Home Office became to a much greater extent than ever before the focal point of police administration. To coordinate, in varying degrees at different times, the development of police services provided by almost two hundred separate police forces in England and Wales, in 1919 there came into being the Home Office's Police Department. This was staffed by civilian administrators—for several years

*Anthony Judge, *The First Fifty Years*, p. 11.

never more than half a dozen—with, of course, the collaboration of H.M. Inspectors of Constabulary.

The First World War had inured Britain to a greater degree of government from the center. Conscription from 1916 until the end of the war had introduced a new element of compulsion into individual lives. The Daylight Saving Act fetched Britons out of bed an hour earlier; the Defence of the Realm Acts laid down the hours at which they could drink alcoholic beverages in bars. Even chief constables were caught in the net of central influences, as when in 1918, at Home Office instigation, they gathered round the table at district conferences, which further encroached on the "island" character of the former dispensation, and formed for themselves a Central Conference of Chief Constables.

Innovations

The inter-war period saw much police innovation. The initiative of individual police officers, many of them working solely within their local jurisdiction, using their force's resources with the support of their police authorities, resulted in considerable advances in the provision of police services.

Among the contributions to police science made by men who came to police commands from outside the police service must be mentioned the *modus operandi* system. This was formulated (no one could be said to have "invented" M.O.—a common sense police technique from time immemorial) by Major Llewellyn William Atcherley, chief of a county force, the West Riding of Yorkshire Constabulary. In 1913 he set up a *modus operandi* crime classification office at his headquarters in Wakefield, which would result some twenty years later in the Crime Clearing House for the North of England being located there. The principle of the system is that criminals may be identified by the mode in which they operate. Atcherley's index classified offenses committed by itinerant criminals on record at New Scotland Yard or at Wakefield, with daily recordings of offenses by persons not registered at either, and a "suspense" record of offenses for which there were no suspects. The classification was based on the type of offense, the point of entry to premises, the means of committing the offense, including the approach, the implements or weapons used, the object or motive of the crime, the time at which it was committed, and the "style"—actual or pretended occupation of the criminal, the story told to ingratiate, accomplices, transport used, and the "trademark"—peculiar acts not incidental to the object of the offense. As the manual states:

> Although it may be possible for a criminal to restrain his actions in the matter of leaving proof of his crime by finger impressions, *no amount of restraint,* or knowledge of the possibility of the results of his crime being recognised as his work, seems to deter the individual from so acting as to render himself unidentifiable by his Modus Operandi.

Major Atcherley served in the army during the First World War, achieving the rank of major general; he returned to the police sphere as one of H.M. Inspectors of Constabulary. The West Riding Constabulary, incidentally, had some five hundred officers serving in the armed forces during the War, sixty-one of whom were killed.

The West Riding force also pioneered police training in the provinces. Atcherley introduced qualifying examinations for promotion from constable to sergeant, and sergeant to inspector, as early as 1913. In the 1930s the West Riding Constabulary Training School began an intensive, thirteen-week course for newly recruited constables. These initiatives were to be models for the later police promotion examinations and the District Police Training Centers.

The advent of the motorcar wrought radical change in police work. The motorist, hitherto a person who regarded policemen as protectors, now came to see them as persecutors, and the proliferation of cars and drivers was in direct proportion to the damage done. The deaths, injuries, and accidents that accumulated as vehicles came from the factories to be driven on roads inadequate to accommodate them, gave police work a new dimension, a new drain on always scarce manpower, and a new and uncomfortable relationship with the public. At the same time, the car gave crime a new kind of property to steal, and a new mobility.

One response to this situation was the institution of police driving instruction, designed to make the police officer the best and most exemplary driver on the road. The pioneer establishment was that of the Metropolitan Police at Hendon in North London, where the commissioner, Lord Trenchard, had the advice and help of the man who was then the world's most famous motorist, Sir Malcolm Campbell, holder of the land speed record. The driving school thus established became a model for similar ones in other parts of the country.

The concept of giving police greater mobility and wider operational scope was furthered in London by the introduction of a body of experienced detectives to go out and tackle professional crime throughout the Metropolitan Police District. The instigators of the "Flying Squad," as it is still called, were Frederick Porter Wensley and Walter Hambrook (its first commander) shortly after the First World War. The success of the squad, known in criminal circles as the "Heavy Mob," has always been based on its mobility, its communications, and above all on its officers' knowledge of criminals—as Wensley said, it "catches thieves because it knows thieves." The principle was later extended on a nationwide scale by the formation of the regional crime squads described in Chapter 8.

The Police Department of the Home Office was headed during the inter-war period by A.L. (later Sir Arthur) Dixon. He had been secretary to the Desborough Committee, and no one could have been better qualified by experience, ability, and character for the job. Among his many contributions to the modernization of the police service was his five-year chairmanship (1933–38) of a committee appointed by the home secretary to inquire into the state of criminal investigation. The Detective Committee's survey was both comprehensive and thorough, and its many recommendations commanded the respect of the service.

They led to the setting up of regional crime clearing houses to cope with the identification of criminals over wider areas than would have been possible for any one force. The business of detective training was taken seriously in hand, the Metropolitan Police and the West Riding Constabulary providing facilities available to police forces at large. Regional forensic science (criminalistics) laboratories were set up, models having been furnished by the Metropolitan Police Laboratory and the laboratory established by the Chief Constable of Nottingham, Captain Athelstan

Popkess. The Home Office also sponsored wireless depots for the maintenance of a national radio network for the police. These common services were funded under a singularly apt adminstrative device, each police authority contributing in proportion to its establishment, the contribution being automatically deducted from the central government's grant. As K.A.L. Parker has pointed out, this was yet another innovation of "that great police administrator, Sir Arthur Dixon."*

All these measures worked to give a new cohesiveness to the service and the traditional operational insularity began to give way as police administrators struggled to meet the needs of a fast changing society, now on the verge of a second world war that would imperil its very survival.

The police had done a fine, disciplined job during the General Strike of 1926. In a potentially revolutionary situation the restraint and good humor that they showed all over the country were a major factor in minimizing the effects of a stoppage which had sought to paralyze industry and communications. An American witness commented: "I have seen more fighting in one night of a local steel strike in Pittsburgh than there has been in all England this week."†

The strike petered out quickly and the police came out of it with great credit, recovering whatever favor they had lost by their own strikes at the end of the first world war.

Trouble in London, in the form of allegations of wrongful arrests, bribery, and corruption, some of which were well founded, aggravated by a press campaign which greatly exaggerated them, soon alienated public opinion, and a royal commission was appointed in 1929 to inquire into police powers and procedures, but its report broke little new ground. At New Scotland Yard, however, a well-liked commissioner, Field Marshal Lord Byng, restored morale and put in hand many measures to improve services. When ill health compelled his retirement he was succeeded by another prestigious military figure, the architect of the Royal Air Force, Lord Trenchard.

---

*K.A.L. Parker, "The Constitutional Structure of the Metropolitan Police," *Police Journal* (January 1981), p. 19.
†Douglas G. Browne, *The Rise of Scotland Yard,* p. 332.

During his period of office the Metropolitan Police hierarchy was in a state of shock. The alarming autocrat, surely diabolically inspired in his ability to identify inefficiency, embarked upon a ruthless program of reform, imposing schemes for rapid and radical reorganization very much more far-reaching than his predecessor's. He introduced an entirely new spirit into the then rather sleepy administration at Scotland Yard, and with the sometimes startled support of the home secretary, and the receiver, Sir John Moylan, set forcefully about the business of revolutionizing the organization (notably in respect of buildings and welfare) and the man management of the force. One of his measures, patently military in conception, was the introduction of a short-service system, intended to rejuvenate the force, whereby men were recruited for ten-year engagements. It did not succeed and had to be abandoned. An equally controversial scheme took better root when Trenchard, again influenced by military examples, applied himself to the improvement of the senior ranks of the force by recruiting better-educated men into them. He was determined that in the long term the force should provide its own officers, right up to the top, just as in the armed services.

Sir Arthur Dixon, at the Home Office, had already tried to tackle the problem of police leadership on a countrywide scale. His scheme, presented to the Police Council in 1929, was to establish a National Police College. This would have a double objective:

> (a) to develop more effectively and bring to the front the men of exceptional qualifications and personality who enter the Police Service on the usual footing, and
> (b) to attract to the service, and so far as possible, to equip for higher posts men of superior education and wider outlook than those who ordinarily joined as constables.*

Not for the first time, Dixon was ahead of everyone else: his plan ran into trouble in the Police Council, where the Police Federation thought it "too much of a short cut to promotion for the favoured few"; the police authorities opposed it on the grounds of expense; and half the chief constables were against it. Lord

---

*Arthur L. Dixon, "The Home Office and the Police Between the Two World Wars." Typescript in the library of the Police Staff College, Bramshill.

Trenchard, however, to whom Dixon had mentioned his scheme, pointing out to him that the Metropolitan Police was big enough to support its own college, seized upon the idea and with characteristic drive and speed founded the Metropolitan Police College at Hendon in 1934.

The instructional program initially lasted for fifteen months, whereafter those who had passed its severe examinations were given a further twelve months' on-the-job training in the ranks of constable, sergeant, station sergeant, and detective (men already serving before entrance to the college were dispensed from the three months as constable), after which they were promoted to the rank of junior station inspector. They therefore had a great career advantage, for in those days it was rare for anyone to reach sergeant's rank in less than seven years and there was little hope of rising to inspector with under fifteen years' service.

The college endeared itself to those who graduated from it, but to few others. One reason for its unpopularity was that a proportion of entrants were selected on the basis of higher educational qualifications or competitive examination, without prior police service (this had not been part of Dixon's plan), and Trenchard intended that eventually no one would reach the rank of inspector without passing through the college. Adverse publicity and opinion within the service vehemently held that a century of police tradition was being discarded (Robert Peel was thought to be turning in his grave), conveniently ignoring the fact that the top posts had always been filled by outsiders—only one man who had joined as a constable had, until that date, risen as far as assistant commissioner.

The scheme did attract some well-educated men who would not otherwise have come into the police, and it *did* provide a short cut to higher rank for promising men already serving. Its main fault lay in the admission of outsiders, for this alienated the service and could well have been done without: the 1930s were a time of economic depression, that infallible stimulant to police recruitment, and many well-educated men were then joining as constables. It should be recorded that Sir Philip Game, Lord Trenchard's successor as commissioner, although coming to the problem with much the same background (a retired air vice marshal, he had been Trenchard's right-hand man in the Royal Air Force), took an entirely different view. He considered that the force could produce its own officers without bringing in direct entrants from outside, although he agreed on the need for bright young men to be brought on quickly. His views on the former point, but not on the latter, were reflected in the planning of the post-war, national Police College.*

In the five years of its existence, the college at Hendon made a remarkable contribution to police leadership, both in London and elsewhere. Among its graduates were two commissioners of the Metropolitan Police, Sir Joseph Simpson, who had joined as a constable, and Sir John Waldron, a direct entrant, and four H.M. Chief Inspectors of Constabulary (Sir Edward Dodd, Sir Eric St. Johnston, Sir John McKay, and Sir John Hill) were "Hendon Men." In all, 191 men graduated, of whom 139 were serving when selected to attend the college. Twenty-one were killed in the second world war; twenty-four left the force after the war; twelve were dismissed, required to resign or reduced to constable; two transferred to the British Transport Police. At one time the six most senior officers of the Metropolitan Police and twenty chief constables of provincial police forces were Hendon graduates. Twenty-seven reached ranks between commander and deputy commissioner in London.†

Lord Trenchard's College closed in 1939 at the outbreak of war. It was not to reopen, but the concept of higher police training had been translated into action. It would not be lost.

British Policing Overseas

As noted in the last chapter, British overseas policing developed in two main styles, the style of the Royal Irish Constabulary and the Indian Police Service on the one hand, and on the other the regular, civil style of Great Britain. Britain's part in the making of the world's police systems during the colonial and imperial regimes was very great—even imperial Rome did not leave such a

---

*See K.A.L. Parker, "Hendon and After," *Police Journal* (July 1980), pp. 219–32.
†Information given to the author by the late T.E. Mahir, G.M., C.B.E., himself a graduate of the college, who reached the rank of assistant commissioner.

considerable police heritage. The Romans relied to a great extent on the legions to provide police services in their provinces (the fighting strength of the Roman army was much reduced by the need to detach men for police duties). The British army's police work was almost entirely confined to major emergencies beyond the resources of civil police to control, such as those in Malaya, where a communist insurrection, based in the jungle, began in 1948; Cyprus, where a rebellion by Greek dissidents in 1955 led to the partition of the island between its Greek and Turkish inhabitants; and since 1969, Northern Ireland.

Nearest to Great Britain of the overseas police forces was the police of Northern Ireland. The Royal Ulster Constabulary came into being in 1922, following the division of Ireland into the six counties of the north and the twenty-six of the south. This force was controlled by an Inspector General (a title inherited from the Royal Irish Constabulary), responsible to the Minister of Home Affairs of the Northern Ireland government. It was supported by a Special Constabulary. Born in troubled times (there was civil war south of the border until 1923), the force has always had to contend with sectarian strife and the Irish Republican Army, a revolutionary organization that is illegal in the republic. The semimilitary style carried forward from the RIC was maintained until recent times.

While Canada's local police forces continued to grow in numbers and size in response to the growth of communities, the Royal Canadian Mounted Police (the name dates from 1920) continued to bear increased responsibilities. Almost two thousand miles of international boundary had to be policed; in 1920 the force was made responsible for enforcing all Dominion statutes; provinces contracted with it to provide their police services— between 1920 and 1950, all provinces except Ontario and Quebec had so contracted. It also fell to the RCMP to operate Canada's Security Service.

An independent federal commonwealth since 1901, Australia consists politically of six states, the Northern Territory and the Australian Capital Territory. Each state has its own system of criminal law and criminal justice, with police controlled at the state level; within the state there are no municipal or other police agencies. The Commonwealth Police Force would be formed in 1960 to perform duties at the national level that could not be performed by the states' police, and supply certain central services, notably the higher training facilities of the Australian Police College. Most Australian police officers routinely carry firearms, but adhere to the home model in the scope of their powers and responsibilities.

New Zealand, an independent dominion since 1907, adopted the home style in 1886, since when the force has not been armed. It has continued to operate as a single national police under a minister of the central government, closest of all the antipodal forces to the Metropolitan Police model.

It is to be expected that in countries that have been largely populated by settlers, as in Canada and Australasia, the police style will differ widely from that found in countries where an indigenous population is ruled by an outside power, as in India and Ceylon. In the former case, the settlers take with them the laws and institutions of the home land; in the latter, law is imposed and is necessarily accompanied by the order without which it cannot be administered. Thus the home police model was adopted in lands where there is general agreement in cultural matters and the semimilitary style proved better adapted to the governance of the others.

The British Empire's territories in Asia, Africa and the Caribbean fall into the latter group and it was along soldierly lines that regular police were established there in the nineteenth century. During the twentieth century, the police forces of British dependencies of all kinds have moved to an increasingly civil mode, while in the larger territories tending to keep some part of their strength in reserve for armed intervention in the case of public turbulence. Ceylon offers an outstanding example of the transition from the semimilitary to the civil mode, an evolution linked inseparably with the names of Sir George Campbell, who reorganized and trained the police along Indian Police lines, from 1866, C.G. Longden, who began to retrain the force for civil police purposes; Sir Herbert Dowbiggin, inspector general from 1913 to 1937, who left behind him an unarmed civil police force of high quality, with facilities for training and resources well in advance of most police forces in the United Kingdom.

This and similar developments took place within the wider context of British colonial administration, which, as Sir Charles

Jeffries has explained,* based its system on establishing each dependency as a separate state with its own apparatus of government: in the long run this had the happy effect of enabling colonies to move to independent status without the revolutions that an overcentralized control of their affairs would surely have caused.

Shortly before the Second World War, the Colonial Office, the ministry of the central government in London which had general oversight of the administration of some forty territories, ranging in size from Nigeria with its population at that time of about twenty-five million, to the Falkland Islands with two thousand, formed the Colonial Police Service. This service was recruited from new entrants to gazetted rank (i.e., assistant superintendent of police, and upwards) and officers already serving in those grades in the various territories, thus providing a standard system of promotion and a capacity for deploying officers where they could be of most service. It also give a career mobility which for those serving in very small forces had been lacking. Membership of the service was voluntary on the part of those already serving or recruited locally; those who joined were liable to be posted anywhere in the countries under the Colonial Office's aegis. During the formative years, it was customary for the gazetted ranks to be filled by expatriate officers while the lower ranks were recruited from the indigenous population, but indigenous officers were gazetted in increasing numbers as evolution towards independence began.†

*Sir Charles Jeffries, *The Colonial Police,* p. 40.
†The origin of the term "gazetted" is the practice of publishing such appointments in the government gazette of the territory or government concerned.

CHAPTER 7

War and Aftermath

The Second World War

Britain in the Second World War came to a greater extent than at any time in her history under the control of the central government. Total war, in which the civilian population was as much at risk as the armed forces, involved unprecedented constraint and direction: conscription—the draft—from the outset; rationing of food, clothing, and gasoline; regulation of industry and commerce; carrying of identity cards; blackout from dusk to dawn.

Aerial bombardment dealt death and destruction as high explosive and incendiary bombs were dropped by massive bomber forces on London, and on provincial cities and seaports. In the latter part of the war new aerial terrors appeared in the form of V-2 rockets and flying bombs. Civilians killed during the war numbered 65,000; the military lost just under 400,000. Many a soldier spent less time under fire than the civilians at home in Britain. The civilian dead included 278 police officers.

In 1939, England and Wales had 183 police forces. It was obvious that they must be coordinated to be able to concentrate to cope with the dire emergencies that might occur anywhere. Power was therefore given to the home secretary to issue orders to chief constables (this was rescinded at the close of hostilities), and arrangements were made for each police force to have at least ten percent of its strength available to go to the assistance of hard-pressed neighbors.

The numerical strength of the police in 1939 was approximately sixty thousand. This was increased by fifty percent, by calling in reserves, creating a totally new War Reserve (the most important step), putting special constables on full-pay service, and much later even conscripting some men for the duration of the war. The manpower situation was aggravated by the enlistment of police officers in the armed forces (twelve thousand of them were in the military at the end of the war), but great service was given, the excellence of the police under fire standing out among the many excellences of the other civil defense corps. Winston Churchill, broadcasting to the nation at the moment of victory, said, "the police have been in it everywhere all the time."

They were rewarded much as they had been during the First World War. In 1945 their pay was at a miserably low level, and it was a time of extra stress, the period of demobilization being accompanied (as it always is) by a steep rise in crime. Police morale was badly impaired, and there was bitter disappointment over the small pay raise that the home secretary eventually agreed to authorize. There was a spate of resignations; 1947 found the Metropolitan Police with some sixteen thousand of their permitted strength of twenty thousand. A Committee of Inquiry was set up under a senior judge, Lord Oaksey; its recommendations regarding improvements in pay gave little satisfaction to the service.

More to the police's liking was the committee's recommendation (implemented in 1953) that there should be a single Police Council for Great Britain, instead of two separate councils for England and Wales, and Scotland, and that it no longer be limited to an advisory function but should become a negotiating body, as between the official side (representing the Home Office and the police authorities) and staff (representing all ranks of the service).

While the service had gained in stature by its work in the war, it gained also from the war by reason of the return of officers from the royal navy, army, and air force. Those who had joined as constables in the years before war broke out came back in 1945 or 1946 with experience that would enhance the post-war leadership of the police—though those who had remained at their posts in war-torn, harassed Britain were in no hurry to recognize this potential. Not a few returning policemen took off the insignia of high military rank to resume their duties on the beat. An outstanding example: Major Walter Stansfield was parachuted into the heart of Nazi-occupied France to lead a Resistance group; he later rose to the rank of colonel, having earned, en route, the Military Cross and the Croix de Guerre with Palms. He returned to his force, the West Riding Constabulary, as a constable, rising through the ranks and being decorated as a Commander of the Order of the British Empire and receiving the Queen's Police Medal for Distinguished Conduct. His final appointment was as Chief Constable of Derbyshire, in which he was honored with a knighthood. Detective Constable Robert Mark, with almost five-years' service with the Manchester City Police, joined the army in 1942, was promoted to major after the Normandy Invasion, and came back in 1947 to resume a police career that culminated in his appointment as Commissioner of Police of the Metropolis. From such men as these, and there were many, the police service gained immeasurably. There was a rare maturity among the coming men of the immediate post-war period.

The Police Post-War Committee; Women Police

To prepare for a post-war change, a Police Post-War Committee had been appointed in 1944, its members being representatives of the home secretary and twenty-one chief officers of police. The committee submitted four reports. In these *inter alia* it recommended the establishment of a national police training system and the wider employment of policewomen.

There had been policewomen for some twenty years. They had proved their worth during the First World War, and in 1919 there were about 150 of them. Despite the recognition by various committees—and even by a Royal Commission—that they had a valuable part to play in police service, the service itself did not encourage their recruitment. In 1939, there were still only 200 women;

three-quarters of the country's forces employed none at all. The Police Federation was no doubt faithfully reflecting the views of its members (and perhaps of their wives) in its disapproval of the whole idea. Women were not elected to their Joint Central Committee until 1952, and then only in an advisory role; they did not obtain full voting rights until 1960.

The work of women police during the Second World War again demonstrated their capacity: the Women's Auxiliary Police Corps numbered 3,700 by 1945, and there were then over 400 policewomen in police forces. Their place in the regular police, clearly, still had to be won; that it *was* won was to a great extent due to one of the serving policewomen. Miss Barbara Mary Denis de Vitré (1905–60) joined the Sheffield City Police in 1928, then commanded by Captain (later Sir Percy) Sillito, a strong and innovative chief. She went to the Cairo City Police in Egypt in 1931, returning to rejoin the home service as Leicester's second (and only) policewoman. In Leicester she began to campaign for the women police and organized national conferences there for them. In 1944 she was appointed to the Kent Constabulary as an inspector by her first chief constable, Sillito, who was then commanding the county force. Her task was to form a branch of women police with a staff of two women inspectors and twenty policewomen. Later that year she was appointed staff officer to H.M. Inspectors of Constabulary; she spent the rest of her time with the inspectorate, where in 1948 the home secretary secured her appointment as an assistant inspector. In that capacity she became the Home Office's and the service's principal consultant in all matters concerning policewomen. A mere enthusiast would never have succeeded as she did in building the women's police service: it was her genuine devotion to the service as a whole that gave her special pleading its cogency. Her open-mindedness, great sense of humor, downright sincere personality, her human sympathy and intellectual grasp, made her uniquely appreciated. Her industry was immense; she visited police forces everywhere, giving constructive advice, making spirited war on the service's ingrained prejudice. When she died at the early age of fifty-four, over 2,600 women were serving as regular police officers in Great Britain. The trend of history was with her, but it is unlikely that the cause of women police would have advanced so fast and so far without her salutary influence.

Training

The Post-War Committee made recommendations at two levels on police training.

First, there should be induction training on a national plan: eight district training centers should be established by the Home Office for recruits (the Metropolitan Police had their own center for this purpose). The centers were to be managed by a committee of representatives from the police authorities of the area, while a committee of the local chief constables would appoint the senior instructional staff and approve the programs. This is yet another example of the partnership of Home Office, police authorities and police chiefs. Recruitment continued to be a matter for the individual forces: the district police training center instructed the recruits sent to them by the chief constables, to whom reports on their progress were made. This arrangement, originally intended only to cope with the post-war influx of recruits, has stood the test of time and is still in operation.

Second, there should be a national police college. This was a tremendous step forward but a great opportunity was, nevertheless, missed. There was no question of reverting to the direct entry from outside as in the Trenchard scheme of the 1930s, but the majority of the committee was firmly against any accelerated promotion for the brightest young officers. They felt it necessary to give an assurance that "the proposed college is not a contrivance for giving undue weight, in the struggle for promotion, to youth, brains, personality, or scholastic proficiency as compared with proved police ability and leadership." This decision had a profound effect on the post-war police service.*

The college originally offered three courses, all requiring residence: six months for sergeants, three months for inspectors, and three weeks for superintendents. The selection of those who should attend was left entirely to the chief officers of the forces concerned.

During its first year, the college began to accept as students officers from overseas police forces, thus making a significant contribution to easing the strain of transferring police power in the

---

*K.A.L. Parker, "Hendon and After," *Police Journal* (July 1980), pp. 229–30.

days of independence for many former colonies and dependent territories. An excellent example is that of the first indigenous Inspector-General of the Nigeria Police, Africa's largest police force, Mr. Louis Orok Edet, who attended the college in those days.

The higher management of the college was in the hands of a governing body on which the home secretary, the police authorities, and the police service were represented; this was chaired by the Permanent Under Secretary of State. An advisory committee, representing the police service, was formed to oversee the programs and make appointments to the directing staff.

Founded in 1948, the aims of the college were stated as being to broaden outlook, stimulate interest, and increase professional knowledge in those reaching the middle and higher ranks. Sir Frank Newsam, first chairman of the governing body, is on record as having said, "The Police College exists to make the Police Service more fully human," and from the beginning the courses comprised both professional and liberal subjects. The first commandant, Brigadier P.D.W. Dunn, with Newsam's powerful backing and the sound advice of F.T. Tarry, one of H.M. Inspectors of Constabulary and chairman of the advisory committee, did great work in establishing the college in the regard of the service. His imaginative leadership and personal qualities enabled the college community to overcome being housed in a depressing former industrial hostel complex (situated at Ryton-on-Dunsmore, near Coventry); he attracted fine senior officers, many of whom rose to chief officer posts, to serve on the directing staff, and he persuaded prominent people from all walks of life to take part in the instructional and social life of the college. Drawing on his army experience, he implanted the "syndicate" system which was basic in military staff colleges: under this system, each course was divided into groups, each of which contained a selection of officers representative of the service backgrounds of the whole student body. Thus, a syndicate would include officers from the Metropolitan, county, borough, and overseas forces, according to their experience in patrol, detective, administrative, and traffic duties. Each syndicate was directed by a member of the instructional staff and constituted a microcosm of the course. The syndicate work lay mainly in prepared discussion and individual contribution; the course as a whole met for other academic and practical exercises. From 1954 the directing staff included an increasing proportion of members from the academic world.

In 1960, the College moved to its present home at Bramshill in Hampshire, some forty-five miles southwest of London. The Bramshill site, nearly 260 acres, with a Jacobean mansion, lake, deer park and woodland, has been developed to provide teaching, residential, administrative, catering, and sporting facilities. It provided from the outset a focal point for the service, where people of all ranks and from all forces could get to know one another and benefit by each other's experience, and has over the years been a major factor in the service's growing cohesiveness.

Dixon and Trenchard's aim of attracting better-educated people into the service, however, was not being achieved. University graduates in the police were rare birds in those days, and substantial as the college's contribution to the quality of police leadership undoubtedly was, the prospect of having to spend several years in the lower ranks before being even considered for selection to attend the college made it negligible as a factor in recruitment. There was concern, too, that the college was training only people already in midcareer. Nothing was being done for the promising younger officers. In effect, fifteen years had been lost before the service, under pressure from the Royal Commission on the Police (1960–62), accepted the concept of picking out the best of the young men and women and giving them the opportunity for early promotion. It was particularly important that—for the first time—selection of such people should be carried out on a national basis.

Therefore, in 1961 it was decided to introduce a special course of twelve-months' duration for constables who had shown potential for advancement. Successful completion of the course would result in promotion to sergeant, and after a year's satisfactory service in that rank, to inspector. The Police Federation, which had been adamantly opposed to Dixon and Trenchard on this very issue of accelerated promotion, now gave its blessing, and Anthony Judge records that "it has had no cause to regret the decision, in 1961, to accept the Special Course as a benefit to the service."*

*Anthony Judge, *The First Fifty Years,* pp. 113–14.

The same year saw the introduction of the Senior Command Course, a six-month program designed to equip rigorously selected officers of the rank of inspector—soon to be superintendent—and upwards for the service's highest posts. In 1965, the college introduced a fourth level of higher training with the Intermediate Command Course for experienced inspectors and chief inspectors, with a view toward preparing them for the divisional and departmental posts held by superintendents and chief superintendents.

Thus, by 1965, the Bramshill courses constituted a higher training spectrum unparalleled in any of the world's police systems.

Consolidation

The Victorians, who initiated regular police forces from 1835 onwards, soon came to be concerned about their number and size. The Royal Commissioners of 1839 recommended nationalization, unsuccessfully; the County and Borough Police Acts of 1839 and 1856 enabled police authorities to merge municipal with county forces, and the Local Government Act of 1882 forbade the establishment of a police force by any municipality with less than twenty thousand population. Six years later, another Local Government Act mandated the merging with the county police of all police forces serving populations of less than ten thousand. Nevertheless, there were still 183 police forces in 1939, some with less than 25 men.

During the Second World War, the home secretary invoked his emergency powers to consolidate and twenty-one small forces lost their identities in mergers with larger ones. At the time this was supposed to be a temporary measure, to be revoked when the war was over, but temporizing tactics managed to avoid reestablishing the former order. In 1946, the bitterly debated Police Act of that year resulted in the compulsory merger of forty-five forces with their county police. The act also provided for voluntary mergers, few of which took place, but by 1960 the total number of police forces in England and Wales was 125.

The Police Act of 1964, which followed the recommendations

of the Royal Commission on the Police which sat from 1960 to 1962 (these are discussed in the next section), provided means for the central government to bring about further consolidations, and in 1966 the home secretary set in motion the reduction of the number of forces to forty-nine. A Royal Commission on Local Government presented a report in 1969, and when its recommendations were implemented in the Local Government Act of 1972, a good deal of readjustment of police jurisdictions had to be made to bring them into line with the radical reorganization which then took place. Six metropolitan counties and forty-seven counties emerged from the old patchwork of local government and the end result for the police was reduction to forty-three forces.

On paper, this may look like progress. Change it certainly was, and it was argued that these larger police forces, none with less than six hundred officers, gave far better scope for effective deployment, general economy and efficiency, and for individual careers. Against this, much of a conservative nature was put forward: the ill effect of doing away with so many independent chief constableships, which small as some of them were, had given the experience of ultimate command responsibility to many more than could have it in the fewer large forces, thus abolishing opportunities for men to grow in the exercise of authority. Though a displaced chief constable might earn more as an assistant chief constable in one of the larger organizations, he now would be only a lesser hierarch under another man's orders. Whether greater size really brought greater efficiency was doubted, when it kept the command too remote from the front line. One major disadvantage was felt in the most important sphere of all—that of the police's relationship with the public. What had taken place since the mid-1960s was a massive dislocation, leaving people uncomfortable with new police deployments that took away familiar figures and severed old relationships. Nevertheless, few with direct experience of the stultifying atmosphere of some of the small borough forces that had survived the 1946 Police Act would, even in the light of experience, wish to see them revived.

The change entailed some loss on the human side of policing and must be seen in the context of a wholesale reshuffling of local government structures, from which the country has yet to recover.

MAP OF POLICE FORCES IN ENGLAND & WALES

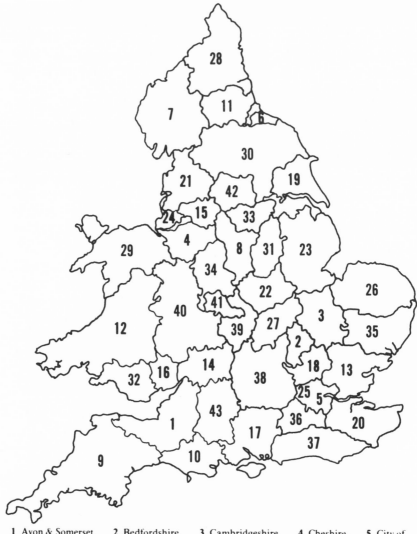

1 Avon & Somerset.   2 Bedfordshire.   3 Cambridgeshire.   4 Cheshire.   5 City of
London   6 Cleveland   7 Cumbria   8 Derbyshire   9 Devon and Cornwall   10 Dorset
11 Durham   12 Dyfed-Powys   13 Essex   14 Gloucestershire   15 Greater Manchester
16 Gwent   17 Hampshire   18 Hertfordshire   19 Humberside   20 Kent   21 Lancashire
22 Leicestershire   23 Lincolnshire   24 Merseyside   25 Metropolitan   26 Norfolk
27 Northamptonshire   28 Northumbria   29 North Wales   30 North Yorkshire
31 Nottinghamshire   32 South Wales   33 South Yorkshire   34 Staffordshire   35 Suffolk
36 Surrey   37 Sussex   38 Thames Valley   39 Warwickshire   40 West Mercia
41 West Midlands   42 West Yorkshire   43 Wiltshire

Reproduced from *Police and Constabulary Almanac*, by kind permission of R. Hazell & Co.

The Royal Commission on the Police, 1960–62

The Royal Commission on the Police, which was appointed in 1960, convened at an uncomfortable time. Police pay had yet again fallen lamentably behind, and there was great discontent in the service, with forces falling below their established strengths by reason of high wastage from resignations and retirements, and from insufficient recruits.

This, however, was not the reason for the appointment of the commission. There had been maladministration of the Cardiganshire police, resulting in the disciplining of the chief constable and the consolidation of the force. Corruption in the Brighton police led to two senior officers being found guilty and sentenced to imprisonment and the chief constable being censured. The Chief Constable of Worcester was convicted of fraud and sent to prison. A minor assault on a boy by a constable in Scotland caused a great furor. In Nottingham the Watch Committee suspended the chief constable, Captain Athelstan Popkess, for investigating whether members of the committee and other citizens were guilty of corruption. Captain Popkess was reinstated in 1959 by the committee at the instigation of the home secretary, but a constitutional point of police governance was at issue. The committee argued that they had the right to suspend a chief constable in whom they had lost confidence. The home secretary relied on the classic view, as stated in the case of *Fisher v. Oldham Corporation* (1930) and other cases: the constable's authority is original, not delegated, and is exercised at his own discretion by virtue of his office; he is a ministerial officer exercising statutory rights independently of contract.*

Dissatisfaction with the conduct of police affairs came to a head in 1959 when the home secretary, Mr. R.A. (later Lord) Butler, was faced with a motion in the House of Commons to censure him for his administration of the Metropolitan Police. A constable, P.C. Eastmond, was sued for damages by a motorist on the grounds of assault and battery, and false imprisonment. The case did not come to trial because the Commissioner of Police, with the Home Office's consent, paid a sum of money in court, which the

*For a critical study of this whole subject, see Geoffrey Marshall, *Police and Government.*

aggrieved driver accepted. The commissioner's refusal to discipline the constable provoked members of the House to argue that if the officer was blameless, then the money should not have been paid, but if he was to blame he should have been punished. Mr. Butler, as always urbanely reasonable, explained that the payment did not imply liability; the question of discipline was one for the commissioner, not for him; and the proof to sustain a disciplinary charge was of a different nature from that required in a civil action. He then took the sting out of the motion by raising general issues—his inability to answer parliamentary questions on the provincial police, the central government's standing vis-à-vis the provincial police authorities, the chief constables, and the Commissioner of the Metropolitan Police, and the relationship of the chief officer and the police force. He mentioned several other matters and informed the House that the time had come for an independent inquiry into the whole business.

The inquiry was entrusted to a royal commission. Fifteen people were appointed to it, the chairman being Sir Henry Willink, M.C., Q.C. One member was American, Dr. A.L. Goodhart, Q.C., Professor Emeritus of Jurisprudence at the University of Oxford. The Royal Warrant of Appointment reads:

> Whereas We have deemed it expedient that a Commission should forthwith issue to review the constitutional position of the police throughout Great Britain, the arrangements for their control and administration and, in particular, to consider:
>
> (1) the constitution and function of local police authorities; (2) the status and accountability of members of police forces including chief officers of police; (3) the relationship of the police with the public and the means of ensuring that complaints by the public are effectively dealt with; and (4) the broad principles which should govern the remuneration of the constable, having regard to the nature and extent of police duties and responsibilities and the need to attract and retain an adequate number of recruits with the proper qualifications.

The commissioners lost no time. Appointed in January 1960, they plunged into a welter of visits and witnesses, and issued an interim report in November of that same year. Their independence was at once apparent—shockingly so to the police authorities—for they did not merely examine "broad principles" but went on to recommend a fifty percent pay increase. Their criticism of previous pay settlements was severe but just: "Awards have done no more than match increases in the cost of living and have tended to lag behind advances in industrial earnings." The commissioners presented the interim report with a keen sense of urgency, having found crime on the increase and police strength fourteen percent below establishment: "The maintenance of law and order ranks with national defence as a primary task of government. It is an essential condition of a nation's happiness. We do not think anyone acquainted with the facts can be satisfied with the state of law and order in Britain in 1960."

In their consideration of the nature of police duty, the commissioners took the classic view of the constable's authority, finding it:

> ...Original, not delegated. On appointment he swears an oath of allegiance to the Crown before a magistrate. It is true that, as a member of a disciplined body, the constable is subject to the orders of his superior officers; but for the way in which he executes these orders he has a dual responsibility: he is to answer to his superiors for any disciplinary lapse and to the courts for any misuse or abuse of authority.... In a country jealous for the liberty of the subject, powers of arrest are not to be lightly conferred or wantonly exercised; and the constable must be vigilant both to use his authority adequately and instantly as occasion demands, and at the same time never to exceed it. We are satisfied that this individual responsibility is more onerous than any delegated to, or assumed by, a member of any comparable profession or occupation.

The report was received without pleasure by the police authorities, who agreed, nevertheless, to find their share of the cost of the recommended award. The effect on the service was highly gratifying: recruitment, on "the gravity of the situation" of which the Inspectors of Constabulary had reported in 1960, was rapidly stimulated, and in 1962 they recorded "the highest annual intake since 1950."

The Police Act, 1964

In its final report, presented in 1962, the commission dealt with its principal business. This was no less than to address the perennial problem of *quis custodet ipsos custodes?** in the form of who should control the police? The commissioners weighed a great mass of evidence from those who spoke up for local control and those who would have the police under greater control from the center, including some who argued for the service to be nationalized. In any event, while conceding the logic of having a national system, the commissioners concluded that the local link should be preserved. One of their number, Dr. Goodhart, refused to sign the final report; he submitted a memorandum of dissent proposing two national police forces, one for England and Wales, and one for Scotland. The commissioners, however, recommended strengthening the hand of the central government in many respects. Their recommendations were nearly all accepted and passed into law in the Police Act of 1964.

This act, the most comprehensive of its kind on the statute books, constitutes the charter of the modern police service. Its recasting of governmental and administrative roles and procedures was so far-reaching that it is necessary to note and consider its provisions at some length.

The local police authorites were reconstituted on a uniform basis. Whether county or municipal, each authority would now be composed of two-thirds members of the elected council for the area, and one-third local justices of the peace elected by their fellow magistrates. The introduction of an element independent of the ballot box into the municipal police authorities marked a considerable change, but the new county police authorities had to make a greater sacrifice: unlike those of their predecessors, the standing joint committees, their expenditures were no longer mandatory upon the county councils: they had to be approved by the latter. Now *all* police authorities' budgets were subject to the vote of the local councils as a whole.

The duty of the police authority is "to secure the maintenance of an adequate and efficient police force for the area." Subject to the approval of the home secretary, the authority appoints the chief constable and determines the strength of the force. It provides buildings, clothing, and equipment. (The arrangement

---

*"Who will guard the guards themselves?" (Juvenal, *Sixth Satire*).

whereby half the cost of the force is met from national taxes continues unchanged).

The police force is under "the direction and control of the chief constable." The latter, however, may be called upon by the police authority, with the approval of the home secretary, to retire "in the interest of efficiency." Appointments and promotions to the office of deputy or assistant chief constable are made by the authority, after consultation with the chief constable and subject to the home secretary's approval. Appointment and promotion of all other ranks are made by the chief constable. Here the municipal police authorities suffered a substantial diminution of their previous powers: the promotion and discipline of the force were transferred from them to the chief constable, while the right of appeal to the home secretary remained.

After the end of each calendar year, the chief constable submits a general report on the past years's policing of the area to the police authority. Whenever required, he submits a report to the authority on specific matters.

A chief constable may provide assistance (e.g., by lending officers) to any other chief constable who applies for it. If in the interests of public safety or order, and such assistance is not forthcoming, the home secretary may direct the chief officer of any police force to provide it. Payment is made by the police authority receiving such service.

A police officer's jurisdiction had hitherto been confined within local territorial limits: it was now enacted that a member of a police force had all the powers and privileges of a constable throughout all England and Wales. A special constable has such jurisdiction only within his own force area.

Consolidation of forces may be made if requested by the respective police authorities and approved by the home secretary. If it appears to the home secretary that consolidation is expedient in the interests of efficiency, and no request for it has been made by the police authorities concerned, the home secretary may order it. The extent to which this section of the act was put into effect has been seen in the previous section of this chapter.

The act defines the police role and powers of the home secretary, virtually the first time this had been done in any statute. His general duty is to "exercise his powers under this Act in such manner and to such extent as appears to him to be best calculated to promote the efficiency of the police." Those powers, as has already been apparent, are formidable. More follows.

The home secretary may require a police authority to call upon a chief officer to retire in the interest of efficiency, after giving the chief officer an opportunity to make representations to him beforehand.

He may require any chief constable to submit a report on any matter concerning the policing of his area, and chief constables must submit a similar annual report to him as to the police authority. The home secretary may cause a local inquiry to be held by any person whom he appoints into the policing of any area.

Regulations as to the governance, administration and conditions of service of police forces may be made by him.

He is the appeal authority in cases where a police officer has been dealt with for a disciplinary offense.

Central supervision of the service was strengthened: the act provides for an increase in the number of H.M. Inspectors of Constabulary, one of whom is to be appointed as Chief Inspector of Constabulary and make the Inspectorate's annual report to the home secretary, to be presented to Parliament. Assistant inspectors and staff officers may be appointed to the Inspectorate.

The act also covers the services that the home secretary is required to provide for the police. These include the police college, district police training centers, forensic science laboratories, wireless depots, a research branch, as well as other organizations and services. It may be recalled here that since 1939, such services had been the subject of a special financial arrangement. As they involved services and the employment of officers outside their force area, a common services fund was established. To this the central government contributes one-half of the cost; the other half, apportioned according to the size of the forces concerned, is paid by the local police authorities.

It is specified in the act that there continue to be a police federation for England and Wales, and one for Scotland, to represent police on all matters affecting their welfare and efficiency, other than matters of discipline and promotion concerning individuals. Regulations may be made for the federations after due consultation with them. The Police Council for Great Britain and Police Advisory Boards for England and Wales, and for Scotland, the former as negotiating body, the latter as consultative bodies, were recognized.

More new ground was broken by making the chief officer of police vicariously liable for torts (civil wrongs) committed by officers under his direction in the course of their employment. Damages awarded against a chief officer in such proceedings are to be paid from service funds; damages or costs awarded against an individual police officer may be paid by the police authority if they see fit to do so.

Complaints by members of the public are to be recorded by the chief officer and caused by him to be investigated; if necessary, the home secretary will request that an officer from another force carry out the investigation. Unless the chief officer is satisfied from the investigator's report that no criminal offense has been committed, he will send the report to the Director of Public Prosecutions. The police authority and H.M. Inspectors of Constabulary are required to keep themselves informed of how complaints are dealt with by the chief officer.

The act lays down penalties for the offenses of assaulting and obstructing police in the execution of their duty, for impersonation of police, and for the illegal possession of police uniform and property. It provides that anyone who causes or attempts to cause disaffection among the police, or induces or attempts to induce a police officer to withhold his services, or to commit breaches of discipline, shall be guilty of a criminal offense, punishable by a fine or imprisonment.

The Police Act of 1964 marks a decisive stage in police development. It reaffirmed the principle of local participation in police governance. It gave Parliament a whole range of subjects on which it can question the home secretary. And it made possible the consolidations of the 1960s.

From Empire to Commonwealth

The era which began with the end of the war in 1946 saw much transformation of the political map of the world. The British Empire dissolved as its vast territories gained independence, though many of the new states chose to remain members of the British

Commonwealth of Nations, a free association of some thirty independent peoples who acknowledge allegiance to the Queen, symbol (as no elective head of government could be) of their community of ideals and interests.

At the present time (1984), a number of territories are still under British tutelage: Anguilla, Bermuda, British Virgin Islands, Cayman Islands, Falkland Islands and dependencies, Gibraltar, Hong Kong, Montserrat, St. Helena and the dependencies of Ascension and Tristan da Cunha, Turks and Caicos Islands, and the British Antarctic, British Indian Ocean, and the Pitcairn Group of Islands.

The general overseeing of their police falls to the Inspector-General of British Dependent Territories Police Forces. Working from the Foreign and Commonwealth Office, London, he inspects all the police forces, but he is also Britain's Overseas Police Advisor, in which capacity he provides the focus for all matters affecting assistance to the police of the independent Commonwealth countries, as well as foreign countries, in accordance with the government's overseas policy.

He thus handles all inquiries on overseas police matters; provides advice on requests for training to be afforded to overseas officers in United Kingdom police training establishments; provides liaison with other countries offering similar police training and development assistance; and is a member of the United Kingdom delegation to Interpol. His liaison functions are many, involving links with the Home Office and other government agencies, and with police forces and training establishments in the United Kingdom.

His work takes him abroad for between four and six months of the year, mainly to the developing countries of Africa, South East Asia, the South West Pacific, and the Caribbean. "If one needed to be convinced of the international brotherhood of police officers, then but a glimpse of my work would suffice," writes the present Police Adviser,* Mr. Robert P. Bryan, a former Metropolitan Police officer of senior command status. Britain, having "lost an Empire" still has a "role," not least in the international world of the police.

*Letter to the author, April 27, 1984.

CHAPTER 8

The Shape of the Service

Strength

The drop in the number of police forces in the 1960s was followed by a large expansion in manpower, which was made possible to a great extent by the pay award mentioned below. In 1964, there were 78,548 regular police in England and Wales; at the end of 1982, there were 120,951. The Metropolitan Police, chronically starved for manpower since the Second World War, was in 1982 only 265 short of its authorized establishment of 26,615 officers. Substantial as this rise in strength undoubtedly was, it still left the ratio of police to population (49,573,000) at about 1 officer to over 400 people.

The increase reflected recognition of the growth of the service's work, with crime, road traffic, and public order, in Britain as in the rest of the Western liberal democracies presenting problems of ever greater magnitude and complexity. "Authorized establishments" were accordingly adjusted. Such adjustments are made by agreement between the police authority concerned and the home secretary. The factors taken into account include: changes in population, incidence of crime, mileage of roads in the police area, number of road traffic accidents, and the length of the police working week (which was reduced to forty hours during the period covered by this chapter).

It is not the practice to grant an increase in establishment unless the force is approximately up to strength. That the new establishments could be filled was due to several factors. The postwar period was one of inflation, with which police pay did not keep pace, and at one time in the mid-1970s, the grave discontent over this resulted in an equally grave loss of manpower. There was even much talk of a police strike that would, of course, have been illegal. A satisfactory formula for pay awards was found in 1978 by a committee chaired by a judge, Lord Edmund Davies, and accepted by the home secretary and the police authorities. This halted the loss of manpower and stimulated recruitment. The Edmund Davies settlement raised police remuneration by almost one-third, and since it was made establishments have been filled.

The unemployment situation was, as always, a potent factor favoring police recruitment, and the post-war expansion of universities and colleges produced a new field of more highly educated young people, many of whom, unlike their fewer counterparts of earlier generations, were prepared to consider a police career. Until the 1970s, graduates* in the service were few and far between, and most of them had earned their degrees after joining the police. At the end of 1982, there were 3,306 officers with degrees in police forces in England and Wales. (In 1982 alone, the number of graduates in the service had increased by 696.) By the end of that year, there were 72 graduate chief superintendents, 31 graduate assistant chief constables, and 15 graduate chief and deputy chief constables.† Of course, the proportion of graduates in the higher ranks tends to rise each year as more graduates enter the service.

Graduate recruitment also was stimulated by a scheme, introduced in 1967, whereby not more than twenty graduates in any

*In Britain, "graduate" implies at least three years of university-level education and a bachelor's degree.
†These figures for progress up through the ranks were compiled by Chief Superintendent Linnane of the Extended Interview Office at the Home Office, and communicated to the author by Mr. K.A.L. Parker.

one year (selected by a rigorous process) could enter the service with a guarantee (subject to satisfactory performance) of a place on the Special Course at the Police Staff College, with its prospect of accelerated promotion after two-years' service.

A perennial difficulty in police recruitment is the age at which a person can be appointed. Reduced from 19 to $18^{1}/_{2}$ years in 1975, in the hope of attracting to a police career the young man or woman who has just left school with *A* levels (the nearest American equivalent is the undergraduate degree), the age of entrance still makes it necessary for most recruits to seek employment elsewhere before applying to join the service.

One school of opinion regards it as highly desirable that young people *should* have such outside experience—experience in being members of the public before becoming police officers; many in the police service believe this. But the recruiting problem nevertheless remains. One solution, given legislative sanction by the Police Act of 1964, was the creation of the police cadet system, under which young people can become civilian members of a police force, continuing their general education while undergoing training to prepare them for regular appointment in due course. The largest of the police cadet schemes was that of the Metropolitan Police. Founded in 1955, by the end of 1960 it had led to the recruitment of over 2,000 constables. The system was reorganized in 1960 as a cadet corps that could be joined at any age between 16 and $18^{1}/_{2}$ years. In 1982 there were 3,881 applications to join from males and 2,780 from females. The nature of modern police cadet training goes far to counter the classic objection that young people were being made "police-minded" too early; indeed, the cadet today, through periods of social service, probably gains more insight into society than those who go straight from school to jobs. With no difficulty in attracting really good recruits, however, the authorities have come increasingly to feel that there is less need for cadets, and policy has been drastically revised. The contribution of the cadet scheme to police recruitment in the lean years, nevertheless, can be hardly overemphasized.

That police establishments are up to strength today has been made possible to no small degree by the number of women entering the service. Of a total of 120,951 officers serving in 1982, 11,015 were women—a steep rise from the 2,651 serving in 1964.

The increase in numbers went hand in hand with their employment in a wider range of duties, including detective work, motor patrol, and accident prevention, in addition to their traditional role with women and juveniles, and regular beat duty.

The Sex Discrimination Act came into force at the end of 1975 and was immediately implemented by the police. Since then, men and women have competed on equal terms for entry to and promotion within the service. It is believed that no other major police system is as far advanced in the employment of women.

The regular police forces of England and Wales are each supported by special constabulary (the special constable has higher status and wider functions than most auxiliary police officers in the United States), private citizens who give up their free time to put on their uniforms and perform police duty. Special constables came into legal existence by a statute of 1662, whereby justices of the peace were empowered to swear in constables, thus constituting a resource from which the authorities could draw in time of emergency: in 1848, when the Chartists massed to present a petition to Parliament, no less than 200,000 "specials" supported the Metropolitan Police (the occasion passed peacefully). Special constables did sterling work during the First World War; filled in for the regular force in the police strikes of 1918 and 1919; assisted during the General Strike of 1926; and made a contribution beyond praise during the bombardments of the Second World War. Today the special constables are less numerous than in the past (the strength in 1982 was 11,932 men and 3,228 women), but they receive more training and go on duty more often than their predecessors.

Feelings about the special constabulary are mixed in the police world. The police authorities are in favor of them; chief officers are glad of the extra strength; at the lower levels there is sometimes a fear that the "specials" will be used to cut down overtime costs and avoid increases in the authorized establishment. From one point of view, it seems incongruous that people—some of whom are trade unionists and stern adherents of the closed shop—should be prepared to work without remuneration: "How would they feel if we went down to their factory and did their work for nothing?" In practice, though, regulars and specials usually get along together pretty well.

The British have civilian-ized many functions formerly performed by police officers; more advantage is probably taken of this resource in Britain than anywhere else. Office work, vehicle maintenance, catering, cleaning—any task patently not needing the services of sworn personnel has been handed over to civilian employees. Traffic duties, notably in connection with parking, now regularly are performed by traffic wardens, male and female, some 4,600 in 1982, and part-time school crossing patrols often are available to relieve police of the duty of "seeing" children safely across the road. The extent of the role of civilians in the modern police service may be gauged from the range of the work they do, some holding appointments previously held by chief superintendents in administrative departments, others acting as scenes of crime or fingerprint officers. At New Scotland Yard, the senior civilian, the receiver (an office as old as the commissioner's) controls a staff of 15,000. The total number of civilians in full- and part-time police employment in 1982 was 41,570.

Structures

The Metropolitan Police District now comprises thirty-two boroughs, and parts of the counties of Essex, Hertfordshire, and Surrey—an area of just under half a million acres, with a population of 7,329,000. The local governments of London, with the exception of the one-mile-square enclave of the City of London, whose Common Council is the authority for the city's police force, do not have the police jurisdiction enjoyed by their provincial counterparts: the home secretary is the sole police authority for the Metropolitan Police District.

Since 1979 the territory has been divided for the purposes of policing as follows: there are four areas, within each of which are six districts; within each district there are a number of divisions (a division corresponds to a police precinct in New York City) and each division contains a number of subdivisions.*

---

*The senior officers in charge at each level hold these ranks: area, deputy assistant commissioner; district, commander; division, chief superintendent; subdivision, superintendent.

Above this territorial organization is the headquarters of the Metropolitan Police, traditionally known by the address where most of its offices are to be found, New Scotland Yard. The command and control system is highly bureaucratic. Rowan and Mayne's headquarters staff was virtually all civilian, and today the police officers at Scotland Yard are greatly outnumbered by civilians. Scotland Yard has civilian staff at many levels and in many specialisms, some under police and some under civilian supervision, though all are answerable ultimately to the commissioner.

The commissioner is the commander of the Metropolitan Police, and on occasion takes personal command of operations. His top police aides number five: the deputy commissioner, who commands the force in his absence, and four assistant commissioners. The deputy commissioner has certain activities under his direct supervision, notably the discipline of the force, including the investigation of complaints (a function parallel with the internal affairs branches of American police forces). He also oversees public relations, the area headquarters, the director of management services, and the inspectorate of the force (the Metropolitan Police has never been subject to inspection by H.M. Inspectors of Constabulary, and like American police agencies, has its own inspectoral arrangements).

The four assistant commissioners and their departments are designated by letters of the alphabet. Assistant Commissioner A is responsible for "police operations," by which rather misleading expression must be understood the work of the uniformed officers, excluding those employed on traffic duties under Assistant Commissioner B. Assistant Commissioner A's sphere is a large one indeed, for in it is the major "police operation" of the force, the patrol, the most ostensible of all police services, the element most in contact with the public at large, and the majority of victims and transgressors. Public order in the Metropolitan District makes tremendous demands on manpower that have to be met from the patrol strength, at the expense of routine preventive policing, and much overtime. London in 1982 had twenty-nine public events that required the presence of more than a thousand officers—one required over eleven thousand. To A Department also falls the protection of royalty, Parliament, and embassies and consulates;

community and race relations; crime prevention; juvenile crime; the Thames Division (the police of the river); liquor and firearms licensing; gaming; the Mounted Branch; the Special Patrol Group (a London derivative of New York City's pioneering of "saturation" policing, it is a tactical reserve force to assist divisional police during exceptional incidences of crime, but not a "riot reserve"); and police dogs.

Assistant Commissioner *B* is responsible for the policing of London's intense traffic and *inter alia* for taxi licensing—London's taxi drivers have to pass a rigorous examination, with the happy result that they can find their way about the city with reassuring competence. *B* Department is also responsible for the increasingly important functions of communications command and control.

Assistant Commissioner *C* is in charge of criminal investigation and has over 3,000 detectives, most of whom are employed in the territorial jurisdictions from area to subdivisional level, the others being in specialist units working from New Scotland Yard. Among these should be mentioned the Flying Squad; the murder, organized crime, anti-terrorist, and dangerous drugs squads; No. 9 Regional Crime Squad (regional crime squads are described in the next section of this chapter); the Metropolitan and City of London Fraud branch; and the Stolen Motor Vehicles Investigations branch. Other responsibilities are fingerprints; the National Identification Bureau; indexes of juveniles, missing persons, and traffic convictions; and publication of the *Police Gazette.* The Metropolitan Police Forensic Science Laboratory and the Criminal Intelligence branch are also under *C* Department, as is the National Central Bureau of Interpol. Scotland Yard acts as the link between all United Kingdom police forces and the Interpol headquarters in France (in 1982, over 51,000 inquiries were made of Scotland Yard by member countries). Finally, the Special Branch is under Assistant Commissioner *C*. Its principal concern is with crimes against the security of the state, subversive and terrorist organizations, watching at sea- and airports, and making inquiries about aliens.

Assistant Commissioner *D* is in charge of Personnel and Training. In his sphere are recruitment, career development, the force's general orders and instructions, and its medical care. Training is a major responsibility: the basic training of recruits, the training of uniformed and detective officers, driving and telecommunications training, and the training of cadets.

The chief civilian at Scotland Yard, with a status equivalent to that of the deputy commissioner, is responsible to the commissioner for the administration of the civil staff as a whole, and directly to the home secretary for the finance and property of the force (in 1982 the force's expenditure was on the order of 665 million pounds sterling, about one billion dollars). Under the receiver come the financial, architectural, engineering, computing, catering, and cleaning services. As previously noted, he controls some fifteen thousand civilians.

The Solicitor to the Metropolitan Police heads the force's legal department, staffed by some seventy civilian lawyers. He is responsible for giving legal advice and overseeing prosecutions. He does not function as a public prosecutor: the decision to prosecute is ultimately the commissioner's.

The Metropolitan Police, by reason of its great size and the mode of its political control, has a "monolithic" character. These two factors combine to insulate it from the kind of questioning at the local authority level that on occasion operates in Britain's other police forces as a check against dysfunction. In recent years, however, increasingly close relationships have been established with the majority of the London boroughs, through formally established consultative committees, and otherwise. This development has been held back in some parts of London by what the present commissioner referred to in his report for 1982 as "a campaign of dedicated denigration of the police." There has also been increased pressure, resisted by the government, for a greater measure of elected, local control of the Metropolitan Police.

The force's tasks, which have increased disproportionately to its strength, have sometimes overstrained a structure that the command and control have failed to adapt in time to forestall disaster. An example of this was the strike of 1918, which nevertheless did not lead to any basic change in the system of command. The major scandal of 1877, "The Trial of the Detectives," when the discovery of corruption at Scotland Yard dealt a severe blow to public confidence, did lead to structural change—a change that established the Criminal Investigation Department as a virtually self-governing enclave whose denizens came to regard themselves as being of a superior order to the uniformed members of the force.

By the end of the 1960s there was a growing awareness of corruption among the detectives, and a feeling that whatever happened they would be whitewashed by their own senior ranks. Investigative journalism by Britain's most respected newspaper, the London *Times,* uncovered an instance of two detectives taking bribes to protect criminals, and from the moment of their trial and conviction in 1972 there was a succession of disclosures that made the disaster of 1877 seem a minor affair. It turned out that the Drugs Squad was acting illegally, giving false evidence and paying informants by "recycling" drugs; six officers were charged variously with perjury and conspiring to pervert the course of justice: three were found guilty of perjury. Far graver was the mischief that had been prospering in the Obscene Publications Squad, where criminals and detectives had developed a lucrative *modus vivendi.* The investigation of their activities resulted in the trial of fifteen officers, two of whom had held the high rank of commander: in 1977 and 1978 thirteen were sentenced to terms of imprisonment.

A new commissioner, Sir Robert Mark, a former Chief Constable of Leicester who took office in 1972 amidst a crisis of public confidence and a general belief that the force was corrupt, determined that only systemic change could prevent such a state of affairs recurring. He also determined that there must be ruthless eradication of the corrupt elements.

The change, destroying the insularity that had been established in 1879 under Sir Howard Vincent, took the form of: a. placing all detectives serving in divisions under the uniformed divisional commander for all purposes, including discipline and assessment for promotion; b. making the deputy commissioner responsible for the investigation of all complaints, including allegations of crime (the latter had been until then the prerogative of Assistant Commissioner *C*); and c. providing for systematic exchange in the future between uniformed and detective branches.

The eradication was entrusted to a new department, under a uniformed commander responsible to the deputy commissioner, staffed by both uniformed and detective officers and working round-the-clock. The commissioner's report for 1974 records that in that and the previous two years 302 officers had left the force by dismissal, requirement to resign, or "voluntary resignation in anticipation of criminal proceedings or to forestall disciplinary action."

It is only fair to add that during Sir Robert Mark's commissionership (1972–77), the Metropolitan Police redeemed the reputation damaged by a small minority of men who had betrayed their trust, especially by superlative performances against "quality" crime and terrorism. Much credit for this must go to the reform and reorientation of the Criminal Investigation Department, carried out by Sir Robert and his Assistant Commissioner C for the critical period, Sir Colin Woods. But much remained to be done, and energetic action has continued under Sir Robert's successors.

Successive reductions in the number of police forces in Britain have resulted in much larger police organizations. The smallest provincial force, Warwickshire, has an authorized establishment of 925 officers, which would be considered large in the United States, while the largest, West Midlands, has 6,684 and employs over 1,600 civilians. The benevolent despotisms of the days when many forces were small enough for the chief to know everyone under his command have gone, and more impersonal systems of command have brought new problems of control and management.

The organization chart of a typical provincial police force shows it to be based on territorial divisions, under chief superintendents, and subdivisions under superintendents, over which is the force headquarters. The chief constable, commander of the force, is assisted by a deputy chief constable, who replaces him in his absence and is responsible for discipline and the investigation of complaints. This delegation to the deputy chief constable of the investigatory aspects of discipline is justified by the fact that the chief constable has to sit in judgment and must not, therefore, be involved in the investigative process. Assistant chief constables deal with departmental and specialist functions. Thus the range of activities under the heading "personnel" are the concern of one assistant chief constable, supervising the recruitment, training, promotion, and welfare of the force. "Operations" are the concern of another, who oversees the work of the uniformed and detective officers, whether at headquarters or in territorial divisions (in a larger force, uniformed and detective operations each have an assistant chief constable in charge). A third assistant chief constable may oversee the force's management services, including its finances, real estate, and general "housekeeping." At the next level down in the hierarchy are chief superintendents, departmental heads, e.g., for criminal investigation, traffic, or operational support, all responsible to the appropriate assistant chief constable.

The number of the latter varies, of course, according to the size of the force. The notional organization described above would have about 2,750 sworn personnel. The West Midlands Police, with 6,684, has six assistant chief constables, with responsibilities as follows: staff services, administration and supplies, crime, organization and development, personnel and training, operations.

"Civilianization" is well advanced in provincial police forces, though nowhere on the same scale as in the Metropolitan Police. For instance, in 1982 the Derbyshire Constabulary had an authorized establishment of 551 civilians, as opposed to 1,767 police.

Horses have been used for police purposes since earliest times. At the end of 1982, 18 forces had mounted branches, with a total of 421 horses, 176 of which were in London. Even in this mechanical age, an officer on horseback has a commanding position from which crowd movements can be assessed and directions given with authority, as may be seen daily in London when the mounted police marshal the large gathering of spectators at the Changing of the Guard at Buckingham Palace, and they have often proved their worth in the dispersal of disorder.

Use is made of dogs by all police forces. In 1982, there were 1,891, of which 415 were in London. The majority of police dogs are German shepherds, but Labrador retrievers and other breeds are used. In the training of dogs and (perhaps even more) horses, the British police have reached and maintain high standards. Labradors in London were successful at over half the narcotics scenes to which they were taken, with the result that 533 arrests were made in 1982. Dogs play their part in counter-terrorism by detecting the presence of explosives. Their general use is for patrol, tracking criminals, and finding missing persons.

So much has been said in this section about superstructure

that it may be appropriate to end it by remembering that the most visible element of the service, the one most at risk physically and legally, is the uniformed constable, working under the supervision of a sergeant, who is responsible to an inspector. The basic structure, on which the whole police edifice rests, introduced by Rowan and Mayne in 1829, has stood the test of time.

Unit Beat Policing

The most salient adaptation of the classic foot beat system was made in the 1960s, and it provides yet another example of how dysfunction generates reform. In the middle of that decade, as mentioned previously, there was a critical shortage of police manpower. Coverage of the regular beats was thin, one officer often having to patrol the ground usually covered by two or three. The constable's work had become dispiriting and monotonous. Calls from the public to police headquarters elicited mixed responses; the few cars available often had too much distance to cover, or too much traffic congestion to cope with on the way.

The run-down state of foot patrol demanded evaluation and experiment. The Lancashire Constabulary gave a lead. Faced with the problems of crime and vandalism in Kirby, a hastily built new town, they found that patrolling in conspicuously marked cars gave far better results than having their officers walk the local beats.

The Home Office Police Research and Development Branch (as it was then called) was asked to work on the problem. A senior police officer, Chief Superintendent E. Gregory, and an operational research scientist, Mr. Peter Turner, were given the assignment. They produced a new formula, based on old principles. Known as "Unit Beat Policing" in the provinces and "Home Beat Policing" in London, the system revitalized uniform patrol and made a valuable contribution to the control of crime.

The original model,* which was to be adapted to local resources and needs, had five objectives: to achieve better rela-

---

*Described by E. Gregory, "Unit Beat Policing," in *Police Research Bulletin* (October 1967), pp. 22–26.

tions with the public by affording closer contact with the police; to provide swifter response to calls for assistance; to raise detection rates by a better flow of information about crime and criminals; to overcome manpower shortage by combining resources; and to make uniform policing more challenging and more interesting.

The territorial unit of the model was a two-beat area, patrolled on a twenty-four-hour basis by a conspicuously marked car. Each of the two beats was manned by a single constable, working an eight-hour shift, at hours approved by the supervisory officer concerned. The area car dealt with calls for assistance; the unit beat officer moved among the community on foot, or in a small marked car (rapidly nicknamed "the Panda"). A detective constable was assigned to the area to investigate crime in partnership with the area car and unit beat officers.

It was a stroke of good fortune that the implementation of the system came at the time when personal radio was coming into general police use; each unit beat officer and the area car were equipped with it. The level of communication improved beyond all recognition and the discretionary patrolling of the unit beat constables produced more and better criminal information. This information was communicated to the final member of the unit beat system, the "collator," an officer located at either divisional or, more frequently, subdivisional headquarters. The collator's function was to centralize local criminal information, collecting it from the unit beat officers, recording and indexing it for communication both to higher specialist branches and within the unit beat system. The collator and his records thus constituted a mini-clearinghouse of local crime. The beat officers could communicate with the collator by personal radio, thus obviating a great deal of paperwork.

The system made the police more visible and more accessible to the public. It gave them far more mobility, both for response and ordinary patrolling, necessitating a massive increase in police vehicles, at the outset by some twenty percent. Greater knowledge of criminals and heightened awareness of local crime led to more crime arrests and vastly increased the pool of criminal intelligence. The uniform officer's new participation in the investigation of crime, added to the greater initiative and individual responsibility to which the system gave scope, quickened the interest and raised the status of the constable. Perhaps most important was the opportunity unit beat policing gave for a constable to be recognized as a local person functioning in and for the community, a renewal of the spirit of the constable's ancient office.

It did not, of course, provide a complete answer to the problems of patrol. The foot patrol on a shift basis is still necessary in areas where the public are present in large numbers, but the extent to which the unit beat model was adopted by the Metropolitan Police and provincial police forces bears witness to the value of this imaginative step forward in following the primary principle of policing—the prevention of crime. During the 1970s the system unfortunately developed excessive emphasis on patrolling in cars, but the recent policy is to return increasingly to foot patrol and closer links with the community.

National and Regional Resources

The uniformity and cohesion of the British police service stems from the national, as distinct from the local, aspects of its administration. The capacity of even the largest force to provide all the facilities necessary for maximum efficiency is insufficient; it is only by pooling resources and entering into cooperative schemes that the service has reached its present level of effectiveness.

The role of the Home Office in this development is capital, and some description of its police dispositions is apposite at this point. The head of the home secretary's bureaucracy, the Permanent Under Secretary of State, like his political master, has police as one of his primary responsibilities. While he is personally active in its administration, the great volume of the ministry's police business is transacted in the Police Department of the Home Office, the coordinating and regulating organism. This Department is under a deputy under secretary of state and four assistant under secretaries of state; it has seven divisions, each under a senior official with the curious title of assistant secretary. A note of some of the matters with which the divisions deal follows:

> F 1 Division: manpower, pay and conditions of service; liaison with the Metropolitan Police *in re* the Home Secretary's role as its police authority.

F 2 Division: police powers and procedures; discipline and complaints.

F 3 Division: operations against crime; police and community relations; research and statistics.

F 4 Division: public order; counter-terrorism; subversive activities; police use of firearms.

F 5 Division: road traffic; police training.

F 6 Division: co-ordination of action in civil emergencies; civil defense; war planning.

F 7 Division: co-ordination of scientific and technological resources.

The central services provided by the Home Office are on a very large scale. One of the most important, the police training system, has already been mentioned and will be described at some length in the next chapter.

The Police National Computer, operational since 1974, provides an on-line service to police forces from central police records: fingerprints, vehicle owners, wanted and missing persons, disqualified drivers, criminal names. In 1982, over thirty-one million transactions were processed, availability being maintained at over ninety-eight percent. The Directorate of Telecommunications, established just before the Second World War, with regional units at different levels, provides a complete operational and advisory service for police, fire, and prison services outside London; the Metropolitan Police is large enough to run its own telecommunications (and criminalistic) system. The Scientific Research and Development Branch oversees equipment and methods, also for the three services. (It was from a Home Office research program that developed the present command and control systems that handle requests for help from the public, the despatching of aid, the recording and monitoring of action, and the storage of information for subsequent management analysis.) The Police Research Services Unit, staffed by police officers, facilitates the transition from research to operational adoption, and provides an information bank service on police research. The Forensic Science Service is staffed by civilian scientists, with a Home Office headquarters and six provincial laboratories. Police officers are stationed at each laboratory for liaison purposes.

In this connection may be mentioned another primary "police" science: medical jurisprudence, the work of the pathologist. There is no central pathological service, but the Home Office recognizes certain experts in the field, many of whom over the years have captured the popular imagination. Famous practitioners of this century include the late Sir Bernard Spilsbury and Sir Sydney Smith, and the most eminent living pathologist, Dr. Keith Simpson, C.B.E., Professor Emeritus of Forensic Medicine, University of London, whose finely written autobiography, *Forty Years of Murder,* gives a richly informative account of his specialism.

Another familiar medical figure on the police scene is the "police surgeon," a local doctor or team of doctors appointed to this position by the chief officer of police. Every busy police station frequently requires the services of a doctor to: take blood specimens in cases of suspected drunken driving; ensure that persons so suspected are not in fact ill; treat prisoners who may be sick, and police or civilian victims of violence; examine persons arrested for drug offenses; certify whether accused persons are fit to appear in court; examine cases of rape and other sexual offenses; and confirm death (in murder cases, a Home Office pathologist is always called in).

The Home Office has a Drugs Branch, staffed by civilians under an assistant under secretary of state, with a London headquarters and three regional offices. The Branch coordinates policy on drugs and poisons, and *inter alia* inspects licenses, maintains an index of addicts, compiles statistics, and collects general intelligence in the field.

In addition to the national police training system, the Home Office also provides a Crime Prevention Center for the training of crime prevention officers, and a center for the training of the instructors and the planning of the curriculum of the district police training centers.

From 1856 dates the oldest of the Home Office's national control devices,* H.M. Inspectorate of Constabulary. The Inspectorate now comprises Her Majesty's Chief Inspector, Sir Lawrence Byford, C.B.E., Q.P.M., LL.B., and five inspectors, all of

---

*From 1856 also dates the annual compilation of criminal statistics. Each police force sends in its figures, which are collated by the Home Office and published by H.M. Stationery Office. The year 1982 had the dismal distinction of a grand total of 3,262,423 offenses known to the police.

whom have previously held appointments at chief officer level. The inspectoral role is far from being merely to report or find fault; Her Majesty's inspectors promote a constructive dialogue with police authorities and chief constables, representing their views to the home secretary and vice versa, and giving much informal advice.

The representative organizations of the service take an important part at the national level. The Central Conference of Chief Constables, established in 1920, is the organ whereby the chief constables can make collective representations to the home secretary and discuss matters within their responsibilities with the minister and his senior advisers. The Association of Chief Police Officers, formed in 1948, represents all the grades of chief officer, i.e., the Commissioner of Police of the Metropolis, the Commissioner of Police for the City of London, their deputy and assistant commissioners, chief constables, deputy and assistant chief constables, and the deputy assistant commissioners and commanders of the Metropolitan Police. It deals with pay and conditions of service, but also concerns itself with wider aspects of police work, operating through specialized committees on such matters as crime, traffic, and communications. The Superintendents Association, dating back to 1920, looks after the interests of chief superintendents and superintendents. The Police Federation, under arrangements already discussed, represents all ranks from constable to chief inspector. All these bodies have their place in the higher administration of the service and no major step is taken without their views being considered. The Federation has used its considerable influence—representing, as it does, the greater part of the service—and shown much initiative not only in promoting its members' pay and conditions of service, also (and especially since the Second World War) in promoting the efficiency of the police. The former Police Council (since 1980 known as the Police Negotiating Board) and the Police Advisory Board, as already mentioned, are negotiating and advisory bodies on which the above associations, the local authorities, and the home secretary are represented.

In turning to the regional services, most of which, as has already been noted, are provided by the Home Office, the most significant development of the past thirty years in the field of criminal investigation was the introduction of regional crime squads. The concept of such squads was not new: the mobility of professional criminals, their trick of living in one police area, committing crime in another, and disposing of the proceeds in yet a third, had already led to ad hoc squads of detectives being formed from neighboring police forces. The natural insularity of detective branches, however, was due for some radical changes. While acknowledging the value of teamwork, detectives had remained more than somewhat individualistic in style; the fact that most crime is local, and their keenness (no one knowing better the havoc that criminals cause) to collar offenders, quite logically restricted their outlook. Changes in the emphasis of professional criminal attack now demanded a wider view.

In 1964, it was decided to build a network of squads of experienced detectives from different police forces on a countrywide basis. Nine regional crime squads were therefore established. The squad for each region came under the general supervision of a committee of the local chief constables; a coordinator, with the rank of assistant chief constable, was put in charge of each squad. Nationwide coordination of the nine squads was entrusted to a committee of chief constables, under the chairmanship of H.M. Chief Inspector of Constabulary, and a national coordinator, with offices provided by New Scotland Yard, as general supervisor of the system. These arrangements have stood the test of time.

Early evaluation of the squads' effectiveness was not altogether encouraging. They were not always getting the quality of detective envisioned; they spent too much time assisting local police forces instead of concentrating on target criminals; the regional criminal intelligence resources were not well oriented. H.M. Chief Inspector's report for 1964 had said that the object was to provide officers who could concentrate on "the ever increasing offences of breaking into premises and on outbreaks of other serious types of crime and to ensure that a well organised mobile team of experienced detectives is immediately available to assist local officers." This was pretty vague.

In 1968, the chief inspector reported that it now had been decided that "the squads should, above all, be regarded as the main striking force concentrating on professional criminals rather than on the investigation of crimes committed." The need for close supervision and good intelligence resources was also emphasized. The chief inspector's report for 1971 reflects real progress in dealing with major criminals; the policy of freeing detectives from the ordinary case load of urban crime was proving sound, and the mobility and communications systems of the squads were being built up to a high level. By 1972, close working relationships had been established with the squads' counterpart in Scotland. In 1974, the report records some of the squads' successes, among them the breaking up of teams of criminals with long-distance operations and the arrest of sixty-one persons at seaports. Squad officers were now being trained in modern surveillance techniques, invaluable in tackling the highly organized enterprises of today's major criminals. The year 1977 saw a ten percent increase in arrests by the squads and the recovery of over five million pounds worth of stolen property. Successful operations against bank robbery and high-value burglary were also recorded. Many of those arrested since the inception of the squads proved to be hitherto successful criminals without criminal records. Only the scope given to the squads made possible the identification of offenders of this kind.

In 1978, the authorities were finally convinced of the need to reorganize criminal intelligence, and a system of regional criminal intelligence offices, based on heavy crime areas, to collate and evaluate intelligence about criminals and crimes, was established in the following year. These offices supply information that supplements that provided by the Central Criminal Record Office in London. Sir Lawrence Byford was able to report that in 1982, "a most successful year" for the squads, "There have been several instances of operations and inquiries extending abroad, with good liaison and co-operation being established with other law-enforcement agencies. The Squads are increasingly involved with gangs of criminals, previously committed to conventional crime, who now attempt to reap the fortunes to be made from the illicit drugs market. Arrests and seizures of large quantities of illicit drugs by the Regional Crime Squads illustrate the effect they are having on drug trafficking."

In many other ways, police forces cooperate at local levels, as in the patrolling of motorways (expressways), where district traffic squads, comprising officers from the forces through whose areas the motorways run, have proved their worth.

The system of mutual aid, whereby chief officers assist one another by the loan of manpower to cope with exceptional demands, has already been mentioned. Since the early 1970s, when the defects of the previously ad hoc system became apparent—the police were in certain instances unable to concentrate men quickly enough to deal with "flying pickets" in great strength—contingency plans have been made to organize police sent on mutual aid in small "police support units," dispatched to areas needing help by a national reporting center, set up when required by the Association of Chief Police Officers. It must be remembered that Britain has no counterpart to the French *Gendarmerie Mobile* or Republican Security Companies (CRS), or the West German Border and Emergency Reserve police forces, or, for that matter, to the United States National Guard. In protracted large-scale disorder, such as that occasioned during the miners' strike in 1984, mutual aid is the only solution short of calling in the armed forces.

The context in which police resources can be centrally and regionally coordinated is far more favorable to the service in Britain than in the United States. It is far easier, for instance, in a country which has a single system of criminal law, where all police officers have common conditions of service and countrywide jurisdiction as constables, and where all have passed through a coordinated system of training, for personnel to be "seconded" for substantial periods from their home forces to duties elsewhere, perhaps in a regional crime squad, as instructors or students in training establishments, or as staff officers with H.M. Inspectorate or in specialist central branches. The progress made since the Second World War in enhancing the professional quality of the police is deeply impressive. This is certainly due in no small measure to the freedom of movement within the service, which gives great scope for the growth of individual and collective expertise.

CHAPTER 9

The Police Career

FOR ALMOST FOUR DECADES no one who has not been a member of a regular police force has been appointed a chief constable. There is now only one way to the top, and this is from the lowest rank. While this has probably discouraged some more highly educated people from entering upon a police career, it has certainly led to the creation of a uniquely comprehensive, in-service training system. Into this system, the newly joined constable is immediately inducted.

To join the service, application must be made to a particular force; it is the prerogative of the chief officer to pass on applicants. Physical requirements must be met, e.g., minimum height 1 m, 72 cm for men; 1 m, 62 cm for women. Glasses may be worn. Age limits are $18^1/_2$–30 years, the latter limit being relaxed in some cases, as for military service. Inquiries are made to establish that the applicant is of good character. A by no means difficult written examination has to be passed, unless the applicant has four GCE O levels—equivalent to a high school diploma. The final decision is taken after interviewing; successful applicants are appointed as constables and make a declaration before a justice of the peace (text in Chapter 4).

The next move is to a residential course of fourteen weeks (sixteen for Metropolitan Police officers) at a district police training center. Here the basic elements of police duty are taught, with emphasis on community relations and human awareness.

The first two years of a recruit's service are probationary; only upon satisfactory completion of this time is appointment confirmed. They are spent mostly on beat duty, during much of which the probationer accompanies an experienced constable. There is a short return to the training center, and the force's varied operations are studied; special aptitudes and interests are noted, with a view toward future employment.

"Pounding the beat," the derogatory term used so often to describe the constable's work, gives a very unfair impression of the recruit's initiation, but it does reflect to some extent a cardinal point of British police philosophy: that the job can only be learned in the presence of the public. For many who join, the beat work proves the most satisfying, and among the seasoned and unpromoted who stay with it are some the finest officers in the service.

Promotion examinations have to be taken by those who seek advancement. Of these there are two, the first leading to the rank of sergeant, the second to the rank of inspector; these are held regularly each year, and there are good facilities for those who wish to study for them. They are not easy: of 10,703 provincial officers who took the sergeant's examination in 1982, only 1,060 passed; of the 4,152 who took the inspector's examination, only 1,310. Passing the examination qualifies one for but does not mandate promotion, which is at the discretion of the chief officer. The days when decisions to promote to sergeant or inspector were a one-man business, however, are over. The practice in all police forces today is to hold promotion boards, and career appraisal is systematically carried on by their personnel branches. There are no promotion examinations beyond the rank of inspector.

Having joined a particular police force does not mean that an officer will need to remain in it for the whole of his or her career. Indeed, those who aspire to posts in the chief officer range are expected to have served in more than one force. The standard conditions of service obtaining throughout the country make it relatively easy to transfer laterally. In the United States, such a transfer usually would involve the interruption of pension ar-

rangements, not to mention the need to adapt to an order of policing probably far different from what faces a British police officer
on transferring. Vacancies are in many cases advertised, to be competed for by those serving on the force in which they occur, and by
others from outside when the vacancy carries promotion.

The chevrons, in the form of a triple *V*, worn on the upper arm
of the sergeant's sleeves, denote the first supervisory rank. As
sergeants in the army wear the same insignia, there has arisen in
the public mind an unfortunate impression that the military noncommissioned officer and the police supervisor hold khaki and
blue variants of the same position. This impression leads to
another unfortunate notion that since the constable is under a
sergeant, he can be equated with a private in the army. From this it
is only too easy to regard the next rank, that of inspector, as being
equivalent to an army lieutenant, especially as both wear similar
shoulder insignia. The question of the distinction between noncommissioned and commissioned rank arises when the onlooker
notices that constables and sergeants salute officers of the rank of
inspector and above in military style. To regard the police rank
structure as akin to that of the armed forces leads only to confusion.
There is no "commission" in the police, except the commission
implied in the office of constable, an office that is held by all police
officers, irrespective of rank. No military officer, not even a five-
star general, has powers over his fellow citizens like those of a constable, and no soldier bears the same burden of individual responsibility to the law for his every official act as a constable does. It
must always be remembered that the great majority of police
decisions are taken by those in the service's front line—the constables and the sergeants.

It could be argued that sergeant is the key police rank, for it in-
volves the supervision of constables and their on-the-job training,
leadership in the field, and a great deal of legal and procedural
knowledge. It has been reckoned by people well qualified to make
such pronouncements that it takes three-years' experience in the
rank to make a good sergeant. The morale of a section depends to
a very great extent on the sergeant's handling of it; a bad sergeant
can cause a lot of wastage. The Central Planning and Instructor
Training Unit in 1977 produced a long overdue training program
for newly promoted sergeants, to be implemented by forces on a

regional basis, with instructors trained by the unit. This came into effect in 1978.

The following year saw a newly promoted inspectors' program, also prepared by the unit, which again trained the instructors. The most usual task for an inspector (like that of a lieutenant in an American police force) is to be in charge of all officers on duty in a particular area for an eight-hour period. Detective inspectors have a shorter supervisory span and their time is scheduled differently. Chief inspectors act as second in command to the superintendents of subdivisions.

Perhaps the posts most enjoyed by senior officers are the command positions in the territorial deployment of the force—the ranks held by commanders of subdivisions and divisions, in London of districts and areas. Once in high rank in the force headquarters, the work is "staff" rather than "line," and only the person at the top of the structure, the chief constable or commissioner, is in command. In a static organization like the police, staff and bureaucracy inevitably come into their own, generating the mountains of paperwork that modern management finds essential.

The identification and training of the service's leaders is associated particularly with the Police Staff College, Bramshill. The college, the national center of higher police training, has often been said to stand as "an act of faith," symbolizing the belief that the service can produce its leadership from its own ranks. It is the natural goal of every ambitious officer to be selected to attend it. Since in any one year over five hundred officers are selected for admission to one of its five long courses, the goal is by no means remote.

In addition to these five courses, the college has instituted a number of two-week courses for senior officers on such topics as "The Police Management of Public Disorder," "Police and Ethnic Minorities," "Finance and Budgeting," and "Research and Planning." In 1982, over four hundred officers attended one of the ten courses in this "carousel" series, which continues today, making the college's services more widely available to a highly influential echelon of the police.

A brief account of the longer courses may be helpful. The Special Course, for outstanding younger officers, lasts for one year.* Selection takes place in two ways. The Graduate Entry Scheme (see pp. 106–107) produces a number; the rest are chosen first by central selection boards that send forward those whom they consider worthy of further consideration to the Extended Interview Board. The board, after $2^1/_2$ days' testing, makes the final selection. In 1982, the central boards interviewed 312 candidates; 99 went forward for Extended Interview; 21 were successful. Of the 39 accepted from the 2 channels, 27 had university degrees. Successful completion of the course carries automatic promotion to sergeant and after 1-year's satisfactory service in that rank to inspector. An outstanding officer thus may reach the latter rank with 6- or 7-years' service. The police are implementing the modern belief that tomorrow's managers must be on the ladder before the age of 30.

The Junior Command Course, selection for which is by the nomination of the chief officer concerned, subject to the veto of the Commandant of the Police Staff College, is a six-month course for inspectors and chief inspectors who may be expected to reach the rank of superintendent. In 1982, 203 officers attended.

The Overseas Command Course, selection for which is in the hands of overseas forces and governments, coordinated by the Foreign and Commonwealth Office in London, is designed for senior officers and oriented to the duties of chief officers of overseas police forces. Three such courses were held in 1982, attended by thirty-seven officers from over a score of territories, including India, Hong Kong, Malaysia, Indonesia, the Caribbean islands, Kenya, Nigeria, Jordan, and Zimbabwe.

The three-month Intermediate Command Course, selection for which is by the chief officers concerned, subject again to the veto of the College Commandant, is designed for officers expected to reach divisional command as chief superintendents or above. In 1982, the four courses were attended by 105 officers, including three from overseas.

---

*The format of the course is to be changed, effective 1985, when it will become a "sandwich" course: three months at the college, then one or two years back on the force, under careful supervision. It will then be decided whether the officer will return to the college as a temporary inspector for a final six months.

The six-month Senior Command Course is designed for those expected to reach assistant chief officer rank and upwards. Selection is by Extended Interview for officers from home forces, and by recommendation of the officer's government in the case of overseas acceptances. In 1982, the course numbered twenty-one officers from the United Kingdom and three from overseas. An important part of their program was the visits made by groups of officers to Berlin, Turin, Rome, Chicago, New Jersey, and Hong Kong, to study and report on inner city policing and such initiatives as multiagency cooperation. A computer-based simulation command exercise was a valuable part of the program.

The Bramshill complex of courses, long and short, since its inception in 1948 has exercised a great influence on the police service. In addition to whatever is learned by way of formal instruction and exercises, the college provides an unparalleled opportunity for the informal exchange of experience and ideas. The fact that the courses require residency gives an extra social dimension, greatly favored by the amenities of Bramshill.

Since 1964, the college has operated a university scholarship program, whereby officers who have shown potential during their courses for higher educational development are able to take paid leaves of absence from their forces to study for university degrees. Tuition and accommodation expenses are paid by the service, and no conditions are attached regarding any obligation to return to duty after three years of study. Early fears that too many might decide to pursue their careers elsewhere were not entirely groundless, but of the 484 officers who were awarded "Bramshill Scholarships" from the inception of the scheme until the end of 1982, only 21 have left the service. The choice of subject is made by the scholar, subject only to the approval of the university. Almost all British universities have accepted students under the scheme, including Oxford, Cambridge, and London, and the range of subjects has been wide, including law, history, politics, economics, adminstrative sciences, English, languages, pyschology, and social studies. Some superlative results have been achieved: in 1982, when fifty-nine Bramshill scholars graduated, seven were awarded First Class Honours, fifty Second Class Honours, and two Third Class Honours. The scheme has considerably enhanced the professional quality of the service. It is now supplemented by

"Bramshill Fellowships," designed to enable officers of any rank to pursue research on matters of concern to the police, under academic auspices. Four such fellowships were granted in 1982.

Since 1971, Bramshill has maintained a faculty exchange program with John Jay College of Criminal Justice, City University of New York, to which now has been added an annual exchange of staff and students with the Academy at Quantico of the Federal Bureau of Investigation of the United States Department of Justice. Mention must also be made of the very successful series of "Police and Language" courses run in turn by France, the German Federal Republic, and the United Kingdom: these provide a six-week, intensive course in the language and police system of the host country. They are attended by twelve officers, usually from the European Economic Community countries. Faculty members travel widely on instructional and advisory missions, and the college attracts a great many visitors from overseas. Its international character, by its continuous acceptance of students from abroad, has been mentioned already.

The college is commanded by one of H.M. Inspectors of Constabulary, at present by Mr. Barry N. Pain, C.B.E., Q.P.M., a former Chief Constable of Kent. He is assisted by a deputy and an assistant commandant, both police officers, a civilian dean of academic studies, and a college secretary, a senior civil servant seconded from the Home Office. The directing staff, as the faculty are called, is recruited from senior police officers and academics. The instructional system was recently (1984) replanned on a four-department basis, grouping the curriculum under social and legal studies, politics and administration, police operations, and police management studies. The first two departments are to have an academic head and a police deputy head; the second two will each be directed by an assistant chief constable with an academic deputy.

The influence of the college on the career structure of the service is obviously great, though only in the case of the Special Course does completion of its courses mandate promotion. Advancement to higher rank is a matter for chief officers of forces, while appointment to the highest posts, those of chief officers of police and of their deputies and assistants, is the prerogative of police authorities, with the necessary approval of the home secretary. Such appointments are advertised in the press by the police authority, and when applications are received a "short list" of names is compiled in consultation with the chief officer of the force. The list then is sent to the Home Office, where one or more names may be deleted, perhaps because the officer(s) in question may not have had sufficiently wide or appropriate experience. It is no longer possible for an officer to rise to the top without acquiring substantial experience in more than one force, except in the Metropolitan Police by reason of its size—and even there the last five commissioners had served elsewhere in senior appointments. This experience both broadens the background and diminishes the risk of undue local influence. The police authority then interviews the candidates on the final list, and subject to the passing of a medical examination and final approval by the home secretary, makes the appointment.

Police regulations provide for an officer to retire on a pension of two-thirds of the final year's salary after thirty years, or on a pension of half-pay after twenty-five years, in the latter case not payable until the age of fifty or when thirty years would have been completed, whichever comes first. Service may continue beyond thirty years, and not infrequently does. For a chief officer the retiring age is sixty-five, but may begin at sixty or earlier if the police authority agrees. With the Metropolitan Police, retirement is at fifty-seven years, except for commanders and above. Tenure, therefore, is of a longer duration than is common in the United States, and far less vulnerable to political or economic change. Any police officer who is dismissed or required to resign by a chief officer or a police authority, respectively, has the right of appeal to the home secretary. There has never been an instance of officers being severed because public funds could not bear the cost; appointment to the office of constable is not "subject to financial ability."

The Commissioner of Police of the Metropolis, appointed by royal warrant on the home secretary's nomination, serves in theory at the Crown's pleasure, but in fact at the discretion of the Home Secretary. As there have only been twenty commissioners since 1829, it may be taken that it has not been the practice to hasten their departure. Four of them resigned, the last in 1918: he was then sixty-eight years of age.

Beyond the chief officers' posts are those of H.M. Inspectorate of Constabulary. These have always been filled in recent times by former chief officers who are appointed by royal warrant on the home secretary's nomination. Their status is civilian; they have no police powers and their function is purely inspectoral and advisory.

From this cursory account, it should be evident that the service offers scope for a wide range of career paths at all levels of its structure, whether in uniformed, detective, administrative, or other special capacities. The system whereby advancement is earned is manifestly fair and open. It may be questioned whether any private concern, however large and opulent, does anything as extensive to develop the abilities of its personnel.

CHAPTER 10

Police Systems Within the United Kingdom

England and Wales

Small as the United Kingdom is in area—94,212 square miles, less than one-fortieth the size of the United States, a little smaller than the state of Oregon—it has not arrived at anything like the unitary police system which most people imagine it to have.

England and Wales form a single area for police administration, but within this, as distinct from the forty-three regular police forces already mentioned, there are many specialist police with limited jurisdictions. The armed services, of course, all maintain police, i.e., the Ministry of Defence Police, the Royal Navy Regulating Branch, the Royal Marines Police, the army's Corps of Military Police, and the Royal Air Force Police. The United Kingdom Atomic Energy Authority also has its own constabulary.

The largest of the specialist police is the 150-year-old British Transport Police. It is responsible for the policing of railways (which are nationalized), the London transport system (subway and buses), as well as the ports and docks that have railway termi-

134

nals. Over two thousand personnel are deployed on the force's missions, which are to protect railway premises and property, goods in transit and passengers' belongings; detect crime and provide general service in the control of traffic in the vicinity of stations; and maintain order and assist the public. The force is organized in eleven territorial divisions (one of which is in Scotland), headed by a chief constable and governed by a police committee, on which are represented the Boards which control the railways, London Transport, and the docks. The force has its own Police Federation.

Among the agencies of the public service that must be mentioned are the investigative divisions of H.M. Customs and Excise, and the Post Office, both of which have long-established counterparts in the United States.

Port and airport police are maintained by the authorities administering the Port of London, Belfast Harbor, the Port of Bristol, Dover Harbor, Falmouth Docks, the Port of Felixstowe, the Isle of Man Airport, Larne Harbor, the Port of Liverpool, the Merseyside Tunnel, Londonderry Harbor, the ports of Tees and Hartlepool, Milford Docks, and Manchester Docks. A National Ports Scheme, in which the regular police of the area concerned cooperate also covers Britain's seaports.

As in the United States, the private security industry, in which many retired regular police officers hold managerial and supervisory posts, has proliferated since the Second World War, manufacturing locks, safes, and electronic protection systems, and providing guard services for business premises, and for cash and goods in transit. Employee screening and store detection have been added to the more familar tasks, such as divorce inquiries. The industry is self-regulating; many firms belong to the British Security Industry Association, which has strict rules for its members, but there has been reason to believe that the quality of some firms outside the association leaves a good deal to be desired in the service they can offer and the people they employ.

It has been calculated that the labor force of the private security industry in the United States considerably outnumbers the officers employed in regular police agencies. It is probable that a similar situation exists in Britain, where some large security companies operate on a scale of manpower comparable with that of regular police forces (and in one case, approximately equal to the sworn personnel of the Metropolitan Police).

The great expansion of the industry began at a time when the police were seriously undermanned, but the main causes of its growth have been the enormous increase in targets for criminal attack and the fear of crime. Though some police officers look with disfavor on the extent to which private security organizations encroach upon the classic police function of protecting life and property, it is obvious that regular police alone could not provide the range of services that the security companies offer. It is only common sense that industrial and commercial firms, like private individuals, should take precautions to protect their personnel and property. And useful as the operation of private security is in the prevention of crime, it is equally useful, by reason of patrolling within the perimeter of an employer's premises, in the prevention of fire.*

Scotland

England became Great Britain in 1707, by the Act of Union uniting England and Wales with Scotland. The two countries had been ruled by the same monarch since the accession to the throne of James VI of Scotland/James I of England in 1603, but not until 1707 did they have a common Parliament in which forty-five members of the House of Commons and sixteen peers in the House of Lords sat to represent Scotland. The Act of Union guaranteed, *inter alia,* the retention of the Scottish legal system, both with regard to its substantive law and the modes of its enforcement.

During the reign of James VI/James I (1603–25), the English offices of constable and justice of the peace were introduced in Scotland. As in England, the constable eventually became a member of a professional police force, but the Scottish justice of the peace did not repeat his English counterpart's triumph over the sheriff. During their long and checkered history, going back to

---

*For listings of security organizations and their services, see *International Security Directory, 1982–83.*

MAP OF POLICE FORCES IN SCOTLAND

NORTHERN
CONSTABULARY

GRAMPIAN
POLICE

TAYSIDE
POLICE

• Dundee

CENTRAL
SCOTLAND
POLICE

FIFE
CONSTABULARY

• Glasgow

• Edinburgh

STRATHCLYDE
POLICE

LOTHIANS &
BORDERS
POLICE

DUMFRIES & GALLOWAY
CONSTABULARY

Reproduced from *Police and Constabulary Almanac,* by kind permission of R. Hazell & Co.

the early twelfth century, the Scottish sheriffs succeeded in keeping judicial functions when their other powers fell away.

In the late sixteenth and early seventeenth centuries, the sheriff's judicial role was firmly established. His prosecutorial role was assumed by the procurator fiscal. This historical nomenclature survives (somewhat confusingly, for its literal meaning is concerned with tax collecting), and Scotland has had a system of public prosecution since 1587.

The nineteenth century saw the establishment of regular police forces (the city of Glasgow can trace a continuous history of its force since the year 1800). In recent times, the number of forces, as in England, has been greatly reduced. There were thirty-three before the Police Act of 1964, now there are eight. Their governance is somewhat different from the English model, in that a statutory police committee of the county or municipal council constitutes the police authority. This committee is not required to have one-third of its members from the magistracy—all are council members—but, like the English and Welsh police authorities, it has to submit its financial proposals to the whole council for approval.

The Secretary of State for Scotland, through his Home and Health Department in Edinburgh, has responsibilities regarding the general efficiency of the police parallel to those of the home secretary in London. National taxes contribute half the cost of the service, on the same conditions as in England; H.M. Chief Inspector of Constabulary for Scotland carries out inspectoral and advisory functions; central facilities, including the Scottish Police College at Tulliallan Castle, are provided by the secretary of state, whose regulatory and disciplinary powers are similar to those of the home secretary.

In England and Wales (at the time of this writing) the decision to prosecute in criminal cases is in most instances taken by the police. It would appear that this is likely to be changed in the near future, the government having decided to introduce a system in some respects like that in Scotland. Some description of the Scottish process may be therefore of particular interest.

Scottish law was profoundly influenced during the Renaissance by the Roman Law of continental Europe, by which time the Common Law had been long established in England. In the French and similar systems on which Scottish procedure was modeled, the mode was "inquisitorial," with the judiciary entering into the investigation and prosecution of crime. The Scottish sheriff, once an investigative officer, by the late sixteenth century was concentrating on being a judge, and the procurator fiscal, originally a "shrieval" official, became the public prosecutor.

Criminal cases in Scotland today are heard in two ways, under either "solemn procedure," when the judges sit with juries, or "summary procedure," when the judges sit alone. At the lowest level are the district summary courts, presided over by lay magistrates, that deal with the less serious offenses. The sheriff courts, where the sheriff sits as judge, may operate under either solemn or summary procedure. The High Court of Justiciary, the supreme criminal court, sits both as a trial court for serious offenses and as a court of final appeal. In the district and sheriff courts, the procurator fiscal is the prosecutor; in the tribunals of the High Court of Justiciary, sitting in Edinburgh or on circuit, the prosecution is in the hands of Crown Counsel, known as Advocates Depute, instructed by the Lord Advocate, head of the judicial system. It is a peculiarity of the Scottish jury trial that three verdicts are possible: "guilty," "not guilty," and "not proven." The Scottish jury has fifteen members and a simple majority suffices for a verdict.

The police role in this procedure is more restricted than that of the police in England and Wales. While the police investigate crime and arrest offenders, they have to report their action to the procurator fiscal of their jurisdiction (Scotland has fifty procurators fiscal), and the case thereupon passes to him to decide whether to prosecute and on what charge. The office of procurator fiscal thus combines elements of the two offices of *juge d'instruction* and *procureur de la République* in France.* While there are advantages in separating the investigative from the prosecutorial function, the Scottish system also has disadvantages. The volume of cases passed to the procurators fiscal by the police places a great strain on their resources, and the drawbacks of the French procedure are by no means unknown in Scotland.

This separation of investigation and prosecution is, of course,

---

*The French procedure is described in Philip John Stead, *The Police of France,* pp. 144–56.

familiar to citizens of the United States. The Scottish system, though, differs markedly from the American, in that the procurator fiscal's is an appointive, not elective, office.

Scotland, although over half the size of England and Wales, has less than a quarter of the population. For 12,303,000 people, the authorized establishment of police strength totals 13,267. The largest force, Strathclyde, with headquarters in the port city of Glasgow, has an establishment of 6,954 officers; the smallest, Dumfries and Galloway, 308.

Apart from their criminal justice limitations, the Scottish police are organized and regulated in much the same manner as the police of England and Wales. Full advantage has been taken on similar lines in the technological sphere; Strathclyde, in particular, has a highly sophisticated command and control system. Interchange of senior personnel is not uncommon. Sir David McNee, Commissioner of Police of the Metropolis from 1977 to 1982, came to the post from the chief constableship of Strathclyde; both H.M. Chief Inspector of Constabulary for Scotland, Mr. Alexander Morrison, C.V.O., Q.P.M., and Mr. I.T. Oliver, LL.B., M.Phil., Chief Constable of the Central Scotland Police, are graduates of Bramshill, and both began their careers and achieved high rank in the Metropolitan Police of London.

One of the minor but highly conspicuous marks of the solidarity of the two systems is the universal adoption of the blue-and-white diced cap band, which has been worn since the early 1930s by Scottish police officers.

Northern Ireland

The Royal Ulster Constabulary, the police force of Northern Ireland, came into being in 1922 following an act of Parliament in 1920 that recognized what are now the Republic of Ireland and Northern Ireland, usually referred to as Ulster. The principal reason for the partition of 1920 was that the majority of the inhabitants of the six northern counties of the island were Protestant and adamantly determined not to be absorbed in a Roman Catholic Ireland. The arrangement has never been a happy one; partitions rarely are.

Ulster's police continued the tradition of the Royal Irish Constabulary (as mentioned in Chapter 6), with its *gendarmerie* style. They were from the outset faced with a double task: the normal preventive, detective, and general duties of a civil police force had to be performed concurrently with the combating of armed subversion and sabotage, from within, and from beyond their own territory as well. Policing Ulster's long border with the Republic was, in itself, a major preoccupation.

The new Republic, after a period of civil war that ended in 1923, and the new Province of Northern Ireland, settled down to mind their own affairs, but the Irish Republican Army—not in any way to be confused with Eire's armed forces—periodically applied itself to forcing the reunification of Ireland by violence. The divided community of Ulster, with its frustrated Roman Catholic minority, proved a fertile ground for their offensive, but the situation from the point of view of the police was well in hand until the mid-1950s. Thereafter, the IRA and other subversive organizations adopted policies of heightened aggression. Both the Irish governments, one in Dublin, the other in Belfast, then imposed internment of known terrorists, and from 1962 there was a period of quiet.

It was not to be expected, however, that Ulster would be immune from the worldwide wave of disturbance and revolt of the late 1960s. Political and sectarian discord raged and the subversionists took full advantage of it. The IRA itself suffered from internal strife, resulting in the emergence during 1971 of a breakaway group bent on the utmost exploitation of violence and terror, the Provisional IRA.

The Royal Ulster Constabulary's semimilitary style had served it well in the border conflicts, with the support of the Ulster Special Constabulary, the "B Specials," but the sudden escalation of urban violence proved too much for its limited resources. The force's authorized establishment was three thousand, but it was not up to that strength when the emergency erupted, and its training had not prepared it for large-scale and protracted, in-city rioting. Consequently, the British army was called to its aid to restore order.

The British Government, in time-honored fashion, appointed a committee under Lord Hunt (of Everest fame) to report on the police. This was only one of several measures taken to put Ulster's affairs on a better footing. The committee's recommendations were accepted by the government and resulted in the force being largely remodeled. The Royal Ulster Constabulary became an unarmed, civilian-type police service with no active antiterrorist role. Attacks on the force by the Provisional IRA, nevertheless, continued, and it became necessary to rearm members for their own protection. The Provisional IRA's offensive had provoked extreme Loyalists to take up arms in their own defense: police and army were thus confronting violence from both ends of the political spectrum.

Meanwhile, the fight was on against both extremist factions. Internment, which had worked before, was tried again in 1971, but this time proved somewhat counterproductive. Emergency legislation was enacted to enhance police powers. Internment was ended in 1975, by which time the security forces had gained firmer control and the reorganization of the police was well under way. It can be truly said that from the years of trial the Royal Ulster Constabulary emerged as a highly professional and effective force.

The outward form was much changed. First, the authorized strength had been far below what the force needed. With less than its original three thousand men—a ratio of one officer for every five hundred people—it had been well-nigh overwhelmed in 1969. By the end of 1983, the establishment had been raised to eight thousand, and recruitment had brought the force up to this figure. The B Specials were disbanded in 1970 and replaced by the Royal Ulster Constabulary Reserve, a body of 4,500 special constables. The force's rank structure and territorial deployment were changed: the inspector-general became the chief constable, and the other appointments and ranks were reordered along mainland lines. The former disposition by counties was replaced by divisional areas, now twelve in number. The training system was intensified, with initial and further courses in communications, weapons, and operational training, and full advantage was taken of mainland training resources at the Police Staff College, Bramshill, of detective training and other specialized facilities.

A major innovation was the creation by the Police (Northern Ireland) Act, 1970, of a police authority (hitherto the force had been directly responsible to the Northern Ireland government) with the same responsibilities as a mainland police authority. The act provides for members of the authority (fourteen to twenty in number) to be appointed by the central government after consultation with representatives of local authorities, other public bodies, the legal profession, trade unions, agriculture, industry and commerce, the object being that the authority reflect the whole community's wishes and fears. Proposals for expenditure are submitted to the Secretary of State for Northern Ireland.

Important as these changes have been, more important is the spirit in which the remodeled force has performed its multiplicity of tasks. The chief constables who have held office during the era of reform, Sir Arthur Young, Sir Graham Shillington, Sir James Flanagan, Sir Kenneth Newman, and Sir John Hermon, have kept steadily before them the absolute imperative of impartial enforcement of the rule of law. Extremists, both Republican and Loyalist, have been treated with equal rigor. An attempt in 1977 to disorganize the province by a general strike, instigated by extreme Protestant groups, was met by strong police measures and the feared disorders did not materialize. In 1983, as reported by Sir John Hermon, fifty-two Loyalist and twenty-three Republican sectarians were charged with murder.

Concomitant with the protracted emergency has been the exploitation of fear by protection racketeers and extortionists. The opportunities presented by terrorism have the double effect of providing the money to keep it going, and making a way of life for predators.

The cost of the emergency is not to be measured in money, but in death and injury. Between August 1969 and December 1983, terrorist action has resulted in 1,646 civilian, 124 Royal Ulster Constabulary, 67 Royal Ulster Constabulary Reserve, and 508 military deaths. Serious injuries have amounted to 4,197 for the police, and 3,898 for the army. Yet the force has carried on with the basic and reassuring routine work of providing police service, extending its community relations program, patiently striving to improve road safety (1983 saw the lowest number of road accidents since 1962), systematically pursuing the investigation of burglary and theft, even increasing its detection rate. It often has been noted, in many parts of the world, that in times of public turbulence routine police duty is neglected. That is certainly not the case in Ulster today.

The solution of the problem of Northern Ireland does not lie in the hands of the police. The causes and course of the emergency are deeply rooted in a tragic history of religious, economic, and political conflict. The prospect of a solution is, nevertheless, improved by what the Royal Ulster Constabulary has done and is doing to maintain the order without which law is irrelevant and democracy a sorry joke.

Islands

The Isle of Man, in the Irish Sea, and the Channel Islands are not constitutionally part of the United Kingdom, being "direct dependencies of the Crown" and having their own legislatures, but it is convenient to consider their police arrangements at this point.

The Isle of Man has its own, very ancient legislature, the Tynwald, whose House of Keys, with the lieutenant governor representing the Crown, governs the island. A regular police force was first formed in 1863. The police authority is the lieutenant governor, to whom the chief constable, commanding the 150-strong Isle of Man Constabulary, is responsible. The style of the force is along mainland lines.

The Channel Islands, which are much nearer to France than England, have belonged to Britain since 1066; they were part of William the Conqueror's Duchy of Normandy. The police system has its roots deep in the Middle Ages, and in Jersey, largest of the islands, the ancient honorary police still function. Each of the twelve parishes has its chief executive, a constable, who is assisted by *centeniers, vingteniers,* and constable's officers, all of whom are elected. A professional police force, some 170 strong, called since 1960 the "States of Jersey Police," has police powers throughout the island, but the elective police officials of the old order operate independently, and they alone are empowered to enter criminal charges and accept bail. It is by no means uncommon for one of the regular police, having made an arrest, to need to fetch the *centenier* from his plow to accept the charge. The chief officer (he is not called a chief constable, which would confuse his office with that of the parish police) is responsible to a police authority, the Defense Committee of the States of Jersey, which consists of seven persons elected by the island's legislature.

The other islands of the archipelago are serviced by the Guernsey Island Police, a regular force to which have been transferred, since 1920, the powers of the old honorary system. The chief officer of the 120-strong force is responsible to a police authority of the same kind as the defense committee in Jersey.

The style of the regular police throughout the Channel Islands is, like that of the Isle of Man, based on mainland practice.

CHAPTER 11

Police and Criminal Justice

The System

The criminal justice system within which the police operate in England and Wales* differs in many respects from the system in the United States. The law itself, while being of the same Common Law family as American law, is unitary, a single body of law operative throughout the two countries. There is no such distinction as there is between federal laws and the laws of the states of the Union. This unitary quality also characterizes the criminal courts, which are organized in a single, pyramidal structure.

---

*Scotland, as has already been mentioned, has its own legal system. In Northern Ireland, the magistrates' courts are presided over by a resident (stipendiary) magistrate, sitting alone. County courts are presided over by judges, with juries for the indictable (the more serious) cases; the judges sit alone to hear appeals from magistrates' courts. The High Court is the supreme court of first instance. The Court of Criminal Appeal hears appeals in cases tried on indictment, and appeals thence lie to the House of Lords. Under emergency legislation, certain "terrorist" offenses may be tried by a judge sitting without a jury. The system of prosecution is somewhat similar to the Scottish, with a director of Public Prosecutions, Crown Counsel, and Crown Solicitors responsible to the Attorney General.

At the base of the pyramid are some nine hundred magistrates' courts, where it is calculated that over ninety-eight percent of the country's criminal prosecutions are dealt with. A very few magistrates' courts are presided over by some fifty stipendiary magistrates—heirs to the Fieldings, professionally qualified justices, located in London and some other centers—but the vast majority are presided over by lay justices, persons who are not required to have professional legal qualifications, and who are unpaid. Of these there are some 21,500 holding the ancient office of justice of the peace. If it is asked (as it must be) how anything as complicated as the Common Law of England can be administered by amateurs, the answer is that the lay magistrates in each court have the services of a professionally qualified person, known as "the clerk," to advise them on law and procedure. The clerk does not participate in judgment. The lay justices usually sit as a body of three or more, the minimum number for trial purposes being two. There is no jury. Improbable as it may seem, the system works. It has the virtue of associating the community with the administration of the law, and the common sense and humanity of experienced laymen have obvious advantages in the adjudication of criminal cases.

There is now no Grand Jury in Britain, another departure from American practice; this ancient Common Law institution was abolished in 1933 and has been little missed.

The magistrates' courts have two very separate functions. They constitute a court of summary jurisdiction, with power to try the less serious criminal offenses, and also to try some of the more serious ones if the defendant wishes to waive the right of trial by jury. The maximum sentence magistrates can impose is usually six-months' imprisonment, but they can commit an offender whom they have found guilty of one of the graver crimes to a higher court for sentencing.

The other function of the magistrates' courts is to conduct preliminary inquiries to determine whether there is sufficient evidence to justify the committal of an accused person for trial by jury in a higher court.

The magistrates also sit on juvenile courts in the cases of persons under seventeen years of age; if the offense is punishable by fourteen or more years imprisonment, the accused may be committed for trial by a higher court.

No judicial office in England and Wales is elective: all judges, at whatever level, are appointed by the Crown on the recommendation of the prime minister (in a very few instances), or by the Lord Chancellor, a political member of the central government, traditionally an eminent lawyer, who is also the Speaker (president) of the House of Lords. The selection of persons to serve as justices of the peace is made by the Lord Chancellor, who is advised by a local committee in each jurisdiction; the committee is careful to avoid a preponderance of persons of any particular political or other affiliation. The lay justices, "the Great Unpaid" as they are called, are in fact chosen from many walks of life, men and women who are prepared to give their time to this very important public service. It is worthy of note that, as a former judge pointed out (no English judge has been removed from office for almost three centuries), "The same tradition of integrity on the Bench appears to exist among justices as it does among professional judges.... There is certainly no case in the last hundred years, where a justice has been charged with accepting a bribe or conspiring to defeat the ends of justice."*

The superior courts, to which reference has been made above, are the Crown Courts. Here a professional judge presides and there is a twelve person jury. The more serious offenses are tried at this level, after committal to it by the magistrates in their capacity of "examining justices" holding a preliminary inquiry.

Appeals from the summary jurisdiction of the magistrates are heard by the Crown Court, when the judge, exercising the court's appellate function, sits without a jury. An appeal on a question of law, however, may be made from the magistrates' court to the Divisional Court of Queen's Bench (a court which in criminal matters confines itself to appeals), where the judges again will hear the appeal without a jury.

Appeals from the Crown Court on a question of law also go to the Divisional Court, but on such questions as conviction and sentencing the appeal falls to the Criminal Division of the Court of Appeal. At the apex of the appeal pyramid, hearing appeals against decisions of the Divisional Court and the Court of Appeal, is the House of Lords, the senior chamber of the legislature, exercising

*Henry Cecil, *The English Judge,* p. 140.

THE CRIMINAL COURTS OF ENGLAND AND WALES

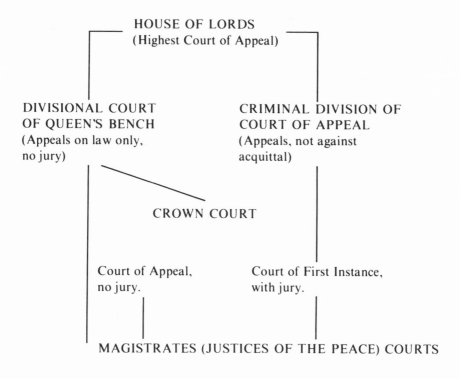

HOUSE OF LORDS
(Highest Court of Appeal)

DIVISIONAL COURT
OF QUEEN'S BENCH
(Appeals on law only,
no jury)

CRIMINAL DIVISION OF
COURT OF APPEAL
(Appeals, not against
acquittal)

CROWN COURT

Court of Appeal,
no jury.

Court of First Instance,
with jury.

MAGISTRATES (JUSTICES OF THE PEACE) COURTS

Summary Jurisdiction,
no jury.

Preliminary Inquiry,
no jury.

its judicial function as the highest court in the land. This is performed not by the House at large but by the judges and persons who have held high judicial office and who have seats in the House. Like the United States Supreme Court, the House of Lords concerns itself with matters of general public importance—it is the ultimate tribunal for the whole of the United Kingdom. As mentioned in Chapter 1, it has no power of what is known in the United States as "judicial review."

The professions of those who practice in the courts are also organized along unitary lines. There are two branches of the legal calling, the solicitors and the barristers. The solicitor is the general attorney, with right of audience largely in the magistrates' courts. The barrister specializes in advocacy, with right of audience in all courts. The two branches are governed by their professional associations, which lay down conditions of membership and administer internal discipline. It is an invariable practice for anyone requiring the services of a barrister to obtain them through a solicitor: a would-be litigant cannot approach a barrister directly. There are far fewer barristers than solicitors—some fifteen hundred in practice, as compared with over twenty thousand solicitors. The judges are invariably appointed from the ranks of those who practice in the courts.

British courts are more formal than American. Magistrates do not wear robes, but in the superior courts both judges and counsel wear wigs and gowns that date from centuries past. To transatlantic eyes, the politeness between judges and counsel, and counsel among themselves, may seem exaggerated: yet, the British trial, at least outwardly, proceeds with a smoothness and decorum surprising to American lawyers. The business of *voir dire,* so time consuming in the United States, is handled much faster, the defense having the right to challenge seven jurors without cause, or all jurors "for cause." There is no right to have an all male or all female jury, nor a jury all of one color. A unanimous verdict is not required: where there are twelve or eleven jurors, and ten agree, or ten jurors and nine agree, the majority verdict is accepted. This goes back only to 1967, until which time unanimity was mandatory. The change was introduced to guard against the possibility that a single juror, bribed or intimidated, might prevent a conviction.

The Police

In an address to the Medico-Legal Society in 1975, Sir Norman Skelhorn, then Director of Public Prosecutions, said:

> It has always been a firmly-entrenched principle in our constitution that in England and Wales a private individual shall be entitled to institute criminal proceedings and that in this sense the enforcement of the law shall be in the hands of the ordinary citizen.... The police in-

stitute the great majority of prosecutions, but in doing so a police officer, with one or two quite minor exceptions, is not acting under any special powers as a police officer, but is doing so in exercising the right of the private citizen.*

This "private" right of prosecution does not exist in the United States (nor, indeed, in Scotland), where all prosecutions are in the hands of public officials. Constitutionally, it helps to emphasize that the police officer is acting as a citizen rather than as an agent of government—one nineteenth-century jurist, Sir James Fitzjames Stephen, went so far as to write that, in the view of the Common Law, a policeman was a person paid to perform as a matter of duty acts that, if he were so minded, he could have done voluntarily. This may have been so in 1883, but the position is different today. While persons other than the police do initiate prosecution—as in many shoplifting offenses—the citizenry by and large show little desire to involve themselves in what they have long ago come to regard as a matter for the police, and since the inception of regular police forces the constable has been given an ever increasing range of duties and powers that are not given to other citizens.

A constable has all the rights of any citizen to arrest under Common Law, with the additional right to arrest if there is reasonable cause to suspect an arrestable offense to have been or about to be committed. English law departed from the ancient division of crimes into felonies and misdemeanours, still preserved in the United States, with the Criminal Law Act of 1967, that listed about a hundred of the more serious offenses as "arrestable." Statute law gives constables powers of arrest in several particular offenses, such as carrying firearms in a public place, or driving while unfit by reason of drink or drugs, and in many cases extends the power to the sphere of suspicion.

It is to constables that magistrates usually issue warrants for arrest, or for entry, search and seizure. These are normally granted by a magistrate sitting alone, upon sworn information submitted by a police officer. Common and statute law, incidentally, authorizes the police in certain instances to enter, search and seize without warrant.

Medico-Legal Journal, Vol. 44, Pt. I, 1976, p. 6.

The point of entry to the formal criminal justice process is, thus, largely controlled by the police. During 1982, some 3,275,000 crimes were recorded by the police; that 1,134,710 of them were cleared indicates the volume of business produced by arrests.

As in the United States, the judiciary has been concerned about the police conduct of interrogation. The key document here is the Judges' Rules and Administrative Directions, rules drawn up by the judges for the guidance, primarily, of the police regarding the protection of persons under interrogation. The rules do not have statutory force but carry the sanction that a judge may exclude evidence obtained without due regard for them. The present rules came into effect in 1964. Like the rules stemming from *Mapp v. Ohio* (1961), *Escobedo v. Illinois* (1964), and *Miranda v. Arizona* in the United States the rules are thought by the police to favor the guilty, and by defense lawyers to favor the police.

The following excerpts from today's rules may be of interest:

> When a police officer is trying to discover whether, or by whom, an offence has been committed, he is entitled to question any person, whether suspected or not, from whom he thinks useful information may be obtained. This is so whether or not the person in question has been taken into custody, so long as he has not been charged with the offence, or informed that he may be prosecuted for it. (Rule I)
>
> As soon as a police officer has evidence which would afford reasonable grounds for suspecting that a person has committed an offence, he shall caution that person or cause him to be cautioned before putting to him any question, or further questions, relating to that offence.
>
> The caution shall be in the following terms: "You are not obliged to say anything unless you wish to do so but what you say may be put in writing and given in evidence."
>
> When after being cautioned a person is being questioned, or elects to make a statement, a record shall be kept of the time and place at which any such questioning or statement began and ended and of the persons present. (Rule II)

The caution is repeated when a person is charged with or informed that he may be prosecuted for an offense, and repeated again with further safeguards if questions are to be put to him after being so charged or so informed. The rules go on to prescribe, *inter alia,* the manner in which written statements made after caution shall be taken. The Home Office then appended the Administrative Directions for police guidance, including the requirements that during questioning a note shall be made of intervals for refreshment.

The directions also refer to the principle, "That every person at any stage of interrogation should be able to communicate with and consult privately with a solicitor." They continue, however, "This is so even if he is in custody, provided that in such a case no unreasonable delay or hindrance is caused to the process of interrogation or the administration of justice by his doing so." One has little difficulty in imagining the reaction of American defense counsel to that.

The British police do, in fact, have wider scope in criminal matters than their counterparts in the United States; an outstanding instance of this is the much greater latitude that they enjoy in connection with exclusionary rules of evidence.

The gathering of evidence to justify a criminal prosecution falls entirely to the police. The scrutiny of the evidentiary proofs of crime by a district attorney, a procurator fiscal, a *procureur de la République* or a *juge d'instruction,* in England and Wales is made by police officers, the decision to prosecute resting in most cases with the divisional commander. In certain instances, however, that decision is not made by the police but by a high official of the central government, the Director of Public Prosecutions.

The director, or "the DPP" as he is generally called in the criminal justice world, is appointed by the home secretary from barristers or solicitors of ten-years' standing; the office dates back to 1879. A staff of lawyers and civil service personnel assists him. Though the office deals with far less than one percent of the criminal prosecutions, it is of extreme importance to the police in particular and to the criminal justice system in general.

First, the director gives advice, as he sees fit, formally or informally, to police and government agencies. Second, some offenses have to be reported to him by the police: some sixty Acts of Parliament specify that his consent must be obtained before prosecution proceedings are begun. An example is the Sexual Offences Act of 1967, where this applies in cases of homosexual offenses where ei-

ther party is under twenty-one years of age. The object of this and
similar statutes is to ensure uniformity in prosecution, in the interests of fairness. The director prosecutes all cases in certain cat-
egories, including treason, murder, manslaughter, obscene publications, and offenses against the security of the state.

Of domestic concern to the police is another of the director's
functions: all cases of complaints against the police by members of
the public have to be referred to him by the chief officer of the
force concerned, unless the chief officer is satisfied that no criminal offense has been committed. This is mandatory—and comprehensive—including minor traffic offenses, as well as such graver
matters as perjury, corruption, and conspiracy to pervert the
course of justice.

Finally, the director is empowered to intervene in, and if he
sees fit, to take over at any stage any criminal prosecution.

Though he is appointed by the home secretary, he is under the
"general superintendence" of the attorney-general, a politically-
appointed law officer of the Crown, Sir Norman Skelhorn, when
Director of Public Prosecutions, liked to think of his office as
that of a kind of "criminal ombudsman." It certainly makes a
great contribution to the quality of criminal prosectuion.

In the magistrates' courts, a police officer may appear in the
role of prosecutor. This is far less common today than in the past;
police forces now often have their own legal branch staffed by civilian lawyers along the Metropolitan Police model, or they avail
themselves of the services of the legal branch of the local government, which will provide solicitors to appear before the magistrates. In either case, the decision to prosecute is made by the
police. In the Crown Courts, once an accused has been committed
there for jury trial, the prosecution is conducted by a barrister.

What has been described in the above section is the role of the
police in the criminal justice system as it has developed since the
advent of regular police forces in the nineteenth century. Change,
however, is now imminent.

At the time of this writing, the British legislators have before
them the massive Police and Criminal Evidence Bill, which *inter
alia* deals with powers to stop and search, and the obtaining of
search warrants; it codifies the powers of arrest, defines the

powers of detention, provides for the treatment and questioning of persons in custody, and reforms police complaints and disciplinary procedures. When the bill becomes law, the readjustment will be far from easy. Also, following a Royal Commission on Criminal Procedure in 1981, the government is drafting legislation that will take the decision to prosecute from the hands of the police and entrust it to a system of public prosecution. Here, too, extensive and far-reaching change is in store.

Whatever the outcome, however, the gathering of evidence will remain with the police, and the setting in motion of the criminal process will still depend upon their inquiries and arrests. Police officers will continue to play their crucial part and find themselves still in what they have long ago found to be the loneliest place in the world—the witness box.

CHAPTER 12

Consensus

IN A LIBERAL-DEMOCRATIC COUNTRY the government does not have at its disposal sufficient force to coerce its citizens into accepting laws and policies that a majority of them actively oppose. This presupposes agreement over what degree of control the government shall exercise. To resolve that issue, countries that are now liberal democracies have in the past resorted to civil wars, revolutions, coups d'état, but the desired consensus (beyond living memory) has been reached in the United States and Britain by an unending, heterogeneous debate—political, social, and economic—at many levels and locations. The history of the British police institution is singularly rich in instances of this perennial process of discussion.

It may be seen in the forums of the legislature, the administrative deliberations of the Home Office and police authorities, the inquiries of royal commissions, departmental committees, and others, and in the proceedings of representative organizations within the police service itself. Sometimes the debate has been timely enough to smooth the path to the future; sometimes it has arisen in consequence of breakdown. Often it has been delayed or

156

protracted; very often it has ended in compromise. But there has been discussion, views have been expressed, and the outcome has been that the police have stayed within the scope of acceptability by the public they exist to serve. A child of British empiricism, if ever there was one, the service has moved to the present day under the impetus of open debate. Perhaps, as the long and heated discussions over the Police and Criminal Evidence Bill have shown in 1983 and 1984, the debate is hotter than it has ever been. And the question of the "accountability" of chief constables, i.e., their relationship with elected representatives, is more than ever to the fore.

The 1980s found the police settled into the pattern that measures taken since the Second World War had designed for it. The reshaping of the structure of the service was, for the time being, complete; the new, large forces had established themselves. Manpower was up to authorized strength; full advantage was being taken of technological progress; techniques of policing were being systematically reviewed and revised. The new decade, though, had brought with it a heightened awareness of the need to regenerate the spirit of consensus, to build up better understanding by the public of the mission of the police, and better understanding by the police of the feelings of the public. The attempts to establish such understanding are sometimes rebuffed by those elements in society who are not prepared to see anything good in the police.

One wearies of the repetition of the words "a changing society," but they are so often spoken because society in recent years has accelerated its pace of change. The American experience of the discontent of minorities has been re-enacted, in miniature, in Britain. Extremist groups seeking violent confrontation are malignantly active. Industrial discord sometimes erupts over-turbulently. Demonstrations of solidarity with a variety of causes sometimes degenerates into riot. Unemployment has left great numbers uncomfortably at leisure. The closer regulation of life necessitated by a large population in a small space makes for alienation from authority. And, like all Western democracies, Britain has to cope with a massive volume of crime.

It all sounds very discouraging. One should remember, perhaps, that nearly everyone has a stake in the good order of the community. The professional criminal is no anarchist: he needs a society in good working order to support his parasitism. The swindling financier takes it much amiss when someone steals his limousine, and the car thief is duly infuriated when his wife has her purse lifted at the supermarket. It is hard to be a criminal, per se, for twenty-four hours of the day; the commonplace business of living has to go on for the transgressor as it has for the law abiding, and despite the welter of wickedness, the world muddles along. It has been calculated that a quarter of the male population commits a criminal offense (more offenses can be committed in connection with an automobile than there are days in the year) before reaching the age of twenty-six, but this does not seem to unduly disturb what André Maurois called "that immense, suspicious, unimaginative mass which composes the English nation."

The police operate in the midst of all this, and their basic reaction is to get on with the job as effectively and impartially as they can. The amount of crime that most alarms the public—street robbery, auto crime, and burglary—is at once a challenge to the service and a demonstration of the need for its existence. By targeting such offenses and concentrating on areas where their incidence is heaviest, the Metropolitan Police, for instance, have had considerable success in reducing it. The home beat system, reinforced by foot patrols and detectives, has had the good effect of giving not only the police more contact with the public, but also uniformed and plain clothes officers more contact with each other.

In London and the provinces the police over the years have been developing relationships with local community associations. This process recently has been intensified, as in the establishment of police community consultative committees in the London boroughs. With regard to race relations, much effort has been devoted to keeping up with a dialogue with minority community leaders. Recruitment of minority members into the police has been more difficult. The temptation to lower entrance standards has rightly been resisted, but well-qualified young people of Afro-Caribbean or Asian origin do not come forward in anything like the desired numbers. One cannot, of course, draft people into the police to secure a representative cross section of the population. Jewish people hardly ever join; Asians seek professional, commercial, or service occupations; the Afro-Caribbeans tend to fear that joining the police will estrange them from family and friends. Some, fortunately, do join, and it is to be hoped that the right kind of recruiting will eventually redress the balance of minority members in the service.

Communication across the board is the name of the game, and it is heartening to learn that the present Commissioner of Police of the Metropolis, like Sir Robert Mark before him, a sincere believer in the open style, in 1984 has been named "Communicator of the Year" by the British Association of Industrial Editors. Addressing that association, Sir Kenneth Newman said:

> In response to justified criticism, my policy will be to answer at all levels of the force with a frank acceptance of error and with an apology where apology is clearly due. Where criticism is unjustified, I serve notice now that we shall be robust in our rebuttal.
>
> The second thrust...will lie in my making every effort, wherever and however possible, to give due publicity to the courage and dedication, the warmth and patience, demonstrated daily by Metropolitan police officers.

The police have had to cope with the development of instant reporting, with its concomitant demands for instant reaction, especially in terms of television. All forces now have press and public relations departments, even if not on the scale of the Information Branch at Scotland Yard, where there is a deputy assistant commissioner in command and professional back-up. Even the press, insatiable as it is, has been known to concede that police arrangements for making information available in recent years have improved. There is still ample scope for dissatisfaction on both sides—by the police with what they regard as unfair criticism and distortion in the quest for scoops, and by the press with what they see as the police making too much of the inhibitions under which they have to operate, notably in relation to proceedings which are *sub judice,* an area in which the United Kingdom's rules are severe indeed compared with the United States' practice in this respect.

At the top levels in British police forces, it is more than evident that the relationship of the service and the public is in the forefront of administrators' minds. Machinery has been created at the lower command levels to maintain the dialogue. Less formal and much less publicized are the initiatives which have for many years been taken by individual police officers, (usually constables) with youth associations. From the county of Cheshire comes the story, in March 1984, of Constable Anthony Cooke, whose sympathy was quickened by unemployed teen-agers telling him they had "nothing to look forward to." Constable Cooke came up with a scheme, "Cop-Out '84," for which he obtained approval from his superintendent, funding from national and local firms, and help from five fellow officers. This enabled him to give the teen-agers an adventure holiday in the mountains of North Wales. Reporting this, *Police Review** commented that in every issue it could give details of many such schemes, and officers performing voluntary services for no reward except personal satisfaction.

Over half the indictable offenses in Britain are committed by persons under the age of 21. Among the measures taken to deal with juvenile delinquency should be mentioned the Saturday Attendance Centers, of which there are over 120, to which many offenders are required by the courts to report. The centers are designed to exercise a reformative influence on persons under the age of 21, by inculcating a sense of discipline and guiding them towards worthwhile leisure activities. Nearly all these centers are managed and staffed by the police. Another important activity is in the cautioning of young offenders who have admitted guilt and who it is believed may respond better to being formally cautioned by a uniformed senior officer in the presence of their parents than by being prosecuted. The scheme originated in the United States, was pioneered in Britain in the 1950s by the Liverpool City Police, and has been generally adopted by police forces. It has been found effective. The Derbyshire Constabulary, for example, cautioned 2,144 juvenile offenders in 1982, as opposed to 2,714 whom they took to court.†

In the final analysis, the standing of the police in the eyes of the people depends on the quality of the service that they provide. Immense progress has been made in recent years in recruitment, training (where humanization has not yet had time to show its full

---

Police Review, Vol. 92, No. 4751 (March 9, 1984).
†Derbyshire Constabulary, *Chief Constable's Report,* 1982.

effect), equipment, and technique. Management sciences have been applied at command and supervisory levels. All this modernization, however, has gone hand in hand with steadfast adherence to British police principles.

Among these the doctrine of minimum force stands very high. That it has been implemented is abundantly evident when the casualties of disorder confrontations are totaled: police sustain far more injuries than rioters. An analysis by Sir Robert Mark of the years 1972–74 shows that in policing 1,321 demonstrations, the Metropolitan Police encountered disorder in 54 of them. On the latter occasions, 49 injuries were reported in the case of persons arrested, 27 to other participants, and 297 to police officers.* Despite the grievous increase of violence against the police, the service has maintained its restraint. The extent of the increase is indicated in the awards made by the Criminal Injuries Compensation Board; in 1972, 3.3 million pounds were paid to victims of crime; 10 years later the figure was 21.9 million pounds, over 30 million dollars. Almost 9 percent of the awards were made to police officers injured on duty.

In 1981 the Commissioner of Police reported 4,444 officers injured in the Metropolitan Police District as a result of being assaulted while on duty; in 1982, the figure was 3,141. In the latter year, H.M. Chief Inspector of Constabulary reported that 6 officers had been killed on duty. While this number is far below that of the officers killed in the United States, it has to be set against the fact that from 1900 to 1981, the total number of officers killed in England and Wales was 77.

The Police Federation, arguing for the restoration of capital punishment for murder, has stressed that in the 18 years before abolition (1965), 11 police officers were killed in Great Britain; in the 18 years since, 30 have been killed. The federation also points out that before abolition, professional criminals largely eschewed carrying guns. By American standards gun control is extremely strict in Britain, but criminals have ways of acquiring firearms, and in recent years have used them more and more often. In London in 1982, shots were fired in the furtherance of crime on 1,060 oc-

*Sir Robert Mark, *Policing a Perplexed Society*, p. 98.

casions, a very low figure compared with big city statistics in the United States, but alarmingly high in relation to those of Britain in the recent past.

In this situation, the police have nevertheless continued to patrol unarmed, but every police force now has a substantial number of officers trained in the use of firearms. These are issued only on the authority of a senior officer, not lower in rank than superintendent. The rule is that such issues shall be made when there is reason to believe that an officer may have to face a person who is armed or so dangerous that firearms are necessary, and they are made only to officers "trained and authorised" to use them. Their use is governed by the principle of minimum force (a principle that is written into the Criminal Law Act of 1967), and officers are individually responsible to the law for their decision to fire.

Another example of the observance of the minimum force rule is in handcuffing practice. Handcuffs are so common a feature of the arrest scene in the United States that it may be surprising to find how little they are used (or even carried) in Britain. Mr. David Powis, Deputy Assistant Commissioner, Metropolitan Police, gives the following advice in a manual written for young police officers:

> Only handcuff prisoners in those circumstances where you would be prepared to swear in court that it was absolutely necessary in order to prevent escape or to forestall unacceptable violence. Remember, handcuffing is degrading and not to be undertaken lightly. Never let a man be photographed by the press when he is handcuffed. If absolutely unavoidable, for example when arriving at an airport or a busy railway station, a raincoat can be thrown over the cuffs to conceal the unpleasant truth. Think on this—an offender is usually a fellow-countryman and, in any event, probably unconvicted at that stage. It is no part of a peace officer's duty to humiliate or shame anyone in their charge.*

Public disorder has severely strained the resources of the police since the later 1960s. In 1968, a year of turbulence in many Western democracies, it became clear in Britain that resort to public protest was being made with a new vigor, and a new violence. Anti-apartheid, the situation in Rhodesia (now Zimbabwe),

*David Powis, *The Signs of Crime*, 1977, pp. 131–32.

the grievances of students, Russia's invasion of Czechoslovakia, civil war in Nigeria, industrial disputes—all those and more gave rise to demonstrations by people sincerely concerned with the issues in question, but who were exploited by such militant foes of liberal democracy as Maoists, Trotskyists, and anarchists. The most prominent of these demonstrations were associated with the war in Vietnam, and at the United States Embassy in London's Grosvenor Square.

On March 17th, a demonstration was called by an ad hoc committee of the Vietnam Solidarity Campaign. Some of those who responded, coming in by bus, were arrested for being in possession of offensive weapons and materials, but several thousand marched from Trafalgar Square to join thousands more in the Grosvenor Square area. There was a violent confrontation with the police as the demonstrators sought to break through the cordon of police protecting the embassy. Fortunately, the cordon held (if the rioters had gained entrance, they would have been faced by the United States Marine Corps guard), but the brutality of the demonstrators had proved a rude shock. One hundred and forty-five police and forty-two demonstrators were injured.

In the period following this demonstration, police tactics for dealing with large-scale disorders of this kind were reassessed and training was reoriented accordingly. On October 27th, the Vietnam Solidarity Campaign and some associated organizations scheduled a march. It was represented to the commissioner, Sir John Waldron, that it would be wise to apply for it to be banned. Sir John, however, was firmly against curtailing the right to peaceful demonstration, and he took pride in his force's capacity to control disorder without tear gas, water cannon, barbed wire barriers, or special riot police. The march attracted some twenty-five thousand participants and proceeded peacefully until a large splinter group, "the October 27th Committee for Solidarity," broke away and headed for Grosvenor Square. There they made violent but unsuccessful attempts to force their way into the embassy: the new techniques of control were effective. Though seventy-five police and forty-five members of the public were injured, the event was seen nationwide as a triumph for restrained and good-humored policing.

The 1970s saw several major disorders. Only too often people meeting to voice some legitimate protest—whether economic, political, industrial, or racial—were joined by members of extraneous political sects who fomented turbulence, and the police often found themselves in the middle, keeping apart extremist groups seeking to do battle with one another. It became clear that lawful protest was being seized upon as a pretext for attacking authority.

The disorder which received most publicity during the 1970s occurred at the West Indian Carnival, held at Notting Hill in London. The carnival already had a bad history of poor organization and crime, in the form of robbery and theft. On August 30, 1976, some 150,000 people had gathered to enjoy the music and dancing, but their day was soon spoiled by large groups of black youths committing robberies and assaults. When the police began to make arrests, the youths reacted with savage violence. Four hundred and eight police officers were injured, as were many spectators, and baton charges had to be made to break up attacking groups. Eighty-nine robberies and 154 thefts were reported. When the view was expressed by some minority oganizations that the police presence in great force had been provocative, and that the affair should not have been policed at all, the commissioner, Sir Robert Mark, made it absolutely clear that there could be no "no go" areas for the police in London.

The injuries inflicted on the police in 1976 caused the force to obtain plastic shields (shields and fireproof clothing are now generally available to the police nationwide), and these had to be used in 1977 when extremist groups were in conflict with one another; even so, in one such confrontation on August 13th, 270 officers were injured. The 1977 Notting Hill Carnival, at which 250,000 people gathered on August 29th, was again the scene of crime committed by roving bands of black youths. Eighty-three members of the public were injured, some with stab wounds, and 192 police officers. Nine hundred and forty-five crimes were reported, including robberies, thefts from the person, assaults on police, criminal damage, burglaries and possessing offensive weapons. Both police and organizers learned a great deal from the experience of these two years, and subsequent West Indian Carnivals have taken place with comparatively little trouble.

The first years of the 1980s brought even more shattering disorders. There was no one cause, and there is still disagreement about the weight to be given to the factors involved, which in fact varied from area to area. As far as the police were concerned the most important new factors in the character of the actual riots were: first, a concentration of unprecedentedly violent attacks on them; second, the use of fire as a weapon and a means for destroying property. The first outbreak of the new type occurred, apparently without warning, in a limited area of the city of Bristol. It was a year later when the most alarming outbreak of the period took place in the Brixton area of the inner city borough of Lambeth, from April 10–12, 1981. This was so severe and caused so much public concern that the home secretary, invoking his powers under the Police Act of 1964, instituted an inquiry. It was held by a senior judge, Lord Scarman, whose report proved a model of analytical and constructive thinking.*

What happened in Brixton must seem tragically all too familiar to Americans; here were all the elements of the formula that had so often engendered disaster in the United States. The scene is the run-down, inner city from which prosperity has drained away—the vacant, vandalized buildings and substandard housing; where unemployment is rife, the educational system has not adapted to the teaching of culturally uprooted immigrants, recreational facilities are poor; where a feeling of being discriminated against possesses young people; and where the population is victimized by opportunistic crime: robbery, auto crime, burglary. And the police (even the American expression is reproduced in Britain) are perceived as "an army of occupation."

The first incident of the disorders, as so often happens when riot flares, was a misunderstanding, in this instance by young blacks, of a policeman's action. What was intended as aid to an injured person was seen as harassment. The animosity against the police, however, was of a general character and needed little to stir it into offensive life. The police, faced with an intolerable level of crime, had taken "saturation" measures to reduce it. A greatly increased patrol presence, with ready resort to "stop and search" powers, had intensified local awareness of the "army of occupation." Given the socioeconomic circumstances, this orthodox police approach was inflammatory.

*Lord Scarman, *The Scarman Report.*

The Brixton disorders proved the most sustained and ferocious that the Metropolitan Police had ever encountered. The restoration of order demanded all the strength available and the protection of property had to go by the board: looting and arson occurred on a large scale. Gasoline bombs, introduced to the struggle by white participation, were used for the first time in Great Britain. When order was at last restored, it seemed that the police had won the battle but lost the war. Two hundred and seventy-nine police officers were injured, and forty-five members of the public. Over a hundred police and private vehicles were destroyed or damaged; damage was done to almost a hundred and fifty private premises, some of which were set on fire.

In July there was a severe outbreak in Southall, a suburb of West London, quite different from all the others, when young Asians reacted violently against what they thought was an invasion of their territory by white extremists. Concurrently, but without any known connection, the most prolonged and at one stage the most intense of the riot series broke out in the Toxteth district of the city of Liverpool; for the first time in Great Britain, CS gas had to be used by the police. This was followed immediately by disorder in the Moss Side neighborhood of the city of Manchester. During the next few days there was much public apprehension about the possible spread of such troubles, and indeed some occurred in various parts of London—including Brixton, the West Midlands, a suburb of the city of Leeds, the cities of Leicester and Nottingham, as well as in Bedfordshire and some towns of the Thames Valley. After that weekend, except in the Merseyside area (Liverpool), where trouble went on until mid-August, the disturbances simply stopped. It is very likely that the rapid spread of rioting was influenced by the impression, given on television in particular, that violence could be embarked upon with impunity, but once the police reaction developed, taking account of the often bitter experience of the riots, order was quickly reestablished.

In the years that have gone by since the tumultuous months of 1981, police leadership in London and in the provinces has responded positively to the harsh lessons then learned, and turned them to good advantage.

Epilogue

IN THE HISTORY of the world's policing, Britain, as this brief study has sought to show, has played a principal part. When one seeks to define her contribution and to see it in the world context, it soon emerges that it is of a dual character. While it is right to say that Britain's police stems from the Common Law, and is distinguished by its localized and civil style, when compared with those countries whose constitutions rest upon the Roman Law inheritance and that have centralized police forces with strong military components, it is not right to leave it at that.

Indeed, from England there spread to America and Australasia the tradition of localized policing, just as from France and Spain spread the tradition of centralized soldierly policing, which took root in many parts of Africa and South America. But Britain, like France and Spain (and like classical Rome), was an imperial as well as a colonial power, and just as they did she found it necessary to secure from above the order without which her laws could not function. Thus, in Asia, Africa, the Caribbean, and in Ireland, the system of police was centralized for each territory along semimilitary lines. The last half century of imperial tutelage saw the policing of the dependent countries evolve from the military to the more civil style, and since they gained independence the general practice has been to maintain centralized civil police with semimilitary reserve components.

The influence of British policing thus has been various as well as vast. What it has in common with that of all liberal democracies is the principle that the police are under and answerable to the laws, guardians of the freedoms the laws guarantee. This sets them apart from the police who in countries with monolithic regimes are the enforcers of an orthodoxy, deviation from which is the highest crime.

Compared with the police of the monolithic states, even the most numerous of the police of the liberal democracies are weak in strength and poor in powers. This is especially true in the United States and Britain. It is bad for democracy to have an overly powerful police, but it is equally dangerous to have a police which is not strong enough. Both extremes are inimical to freedom—the balance has to be vigilantly kept.

Whether the Western-style democracies have provided themselves with a sufficiency of police protection is questionable. Crime, a squalid nuisance today, seems likely to be something worse tomorrow, as organized criminal associations step up their exploitation of human frailties and fears, corruption and peculation corrode business and public life, rising opportunistic delinquency preys upon all and sundry, and fanatical terrorism takes advantage of the ever greater vulnerability of civilized society. Nations can be overcome from within, just as they can be overcome by war. The strength, character and purpose of the police systems they develop is crucial to their well-being, even to their continuance.

Britain's old dominion "over palm and pine" has passed, but much that was good in it survives, not least in the police systems of lands now independent. It is good to see that British police training still has a great international clientele, and good, too, to see how outreaching the service has now become in its relations with police overseas. At home the tradition of professional policing is stronger than ever. With the new leadership which has risen from the ranks of the service, and the quality of the people in it, there are good grounds for confidence in its capacity to cope with the problems that the future most assuredly has in store.

Bibliography

ADAM, J. COLLYER. See Gross, Hans.

ALDERSON, J.C., AND PHILIP JOHN STEAD. *The Police We Deserve.* London: Wolfe, 1973.

ALDERSON, JOHN. *Policing Freedom: A Commentary on the Dilemmas of Policing in Western Democracies.* Estoven, Plymouth: Macdonald and Evans, 1979.

ALLEN, R.J. *Effective Supervision in the Police Service.* London: McGraw-Hill, 1978.

ASCOLI, DAVID. *The Queen's Peace: The Origins and Development of the Metropolitan Police, 1829–1979.* London: Hamish Hamilton, 1979.

ATCHERLEY, SIR LLEWELLYN WILLIAM. *M.O. Modus Operandi: Criminal Investigation and Detection.* 1913. Leeds: Charley and Pickersgill, 1937.

BABINGTON, ANTHONY. *A House in Bow Street: Crime and the Magistracy. London, 1740–1881.* London: Macdonald, 1969.

———. *The Rule of Law in Britain from the Roman Occupation to the Present Day.* Chichester and London: Barry Rose, 1978.

BANTON, MICHAEL. *The Policeman in the Community.* London: Tavistock, 1964.

————. *Police Community Relations*. London: Collins, 1972.

BRADY, CONOR: *Guardians of the Peace*. Dublin: Gill and Macmillan, 1974.

BREATHNACH, SEAMUS. *The Irish Police: From Earliest Times to the Present Day*. Dublin: Anvil Books, 1974.

BROWNE, DOUGLAS G. *The Rise of Scotland Yard: A History of the Metropolitan Police*. London: George G. Harrap, 1956.

BUNN, FRANK LEONARD. *No Silver Spoon*. Stoke-on-Trent: F.L. Bunn, 1970.

BUNYARD, R.S. *Police Management Handbook*. London: McGraw-Hill, 1979.

CAIN, MAUREEN E.: *Society and the Policeman's Role*. London and Boston: Routledge and Kegan Paul, 1973.

CAVENAGH, T.A. *Scotland Yard Past and Present*. London, 1892.

CECIL, HENRY. *The English Judge*. London: Stevens, 1970.

CENTRAL OFFICE OF INFORMATION. *Criminal Justice in Britain*. London: HMSO., 1975.

CLARK, ERLAND FENN. *Truncheons: Their Romance and Reality*. London: Herbert Jenkins, 1935.

COATMAN, JOHN. *Police*. London: Oxford University Press, 1959.

COBB, BELTON. *Critical Years at the Yard: The Career of Frederick Williamson of the Detective Department and the CID*. London: Faber and Faber, 1957.

————. *The First Detectives: And the Early Career of Richard Mayne, Commissioner of Police*. London: Faber and Faber, 1957.

————: *Murdered on Duty: A Chronicle of the Killing of Policemen*. London: Brown Watson, 1966.

COLLINS, PHILIP. *Dickens and Crime* (1962). Bloomington: Indiana University Press, 1968.

COLQUHOUN, PATRICK. *A Treatise on the Police of the Metropolis*. (London, 1795). Reprint of 7th ed., 1806. Montclair, NJ: Patterson Smith, 1969.

————. *A Treatise on the Commerce and Police of the River Thames*. (London, 1800). Reprint ed. Montclair, NJ: Patterson Smith, 1971.

————. *A Treatise on Indigence*. London, 1806.

COX, BARRY, JOHN SHIRLEY AND MARTIN SHORT. *The Fall of Scotland Yard*. Harmondsworth: Penguin, 1977.

CRAMER, JAMES. *The World's Police*. London: Cassell, 1964.

CRITCHLEY, T.A. *A History of Police in England and Wales.* (1967). Rev. ed. London: Constable, 1978.

———. *The Conquest of Violence: Order and Liberty in Britain.* London: Constable, 1970.

CRONIN, JOHN J. "The Fingerprinters." In Stead, Philip John (Ed.), *Pioneers in Policing.* Montclair, NJ: Patterson Smith, 1977; London: McGraw-Hill, 1977.

CURRY, J.C. *The Indian Police.* London: Faber and Faber, 1932.

DAVIES, R.W. "Police Work in Roman Times." In *History Today,* 1968.

DE VEIL, THOMAS. *Observations on the Practice of a Justice of the Peace.* (London, 1747).

DILNOT, GEORGE (Ed.). *The Trial of the Detectives.* London: Geoffrey Bles, 1928.

ELMES, FRANK. "Police in Modern Society." In Morland, Nigel (Ed.), *The Criminologist.* London: Wolfe, 1971.

ENGLISH, J., AND R. HOUGHTON. *Police Training Manual* (1975). 4th ed. London: McGraw-Hill, 1983.

EVANS, PETER. *The Police Revolution.* London: Allen and Unwin, 1974

FIELDING, HENRY. *An Inquiry into the Late Increase of Robbers etc.* London: 1751.

———. *The Journal of a Voyage to Lisbon.* London: 1755.

FIELDING, SIR JOHN. *An Account of the Origin and Effects of a Police Set on Foot by His Grace the Duke of Newcastle in the Year* 1753, *upon a Plan presented to His Grace by the late Henry Fielding, Esq.* London: 1758.

FOSDICK, RAYMOND B. *European Police Systems* (1915). Reprint ed. Montclair: Patterson Smith, 1969

———. *American Police Systems* (1920). Reprint ed. Montclair: Patterson Smith, 1969.

GAY, WILLIAM O. *Communications and Crime.* London: Barry Rose, 1973.

GRANT, DOUGLAS. *The Thin Blue Line. The Story of the City of Glasgow Police.* London: John Long, 1973.

GRASSBERGER, ROLAND. "Hans Gross" in Mannheim, Herman (ed). *Pioneers in Criminology* (1960). 2nd ed. Montclair: Patterson Smith, 1972.

GRIFFITHS, SIR PERCIVAL. *To Guard my People. The History of the Indian Police.* London: Ernest Benn, 1971.

GRIGG, MARY. *The Challenor Case.* Harmondsworth: Penguin, 1965.

GROSS, HANS. *Criminal Investigation. A Practical Textbook for Magistrates, Police Officers and Lawyers. Adapted from the System der Kriminalistik of Dr Hans Gross by J. Collyer Adam* (1906). 2nd ed. London: Sweet and Maxwell, 1924.

GUPTA, ANANDSWARUP. *The Police in British India 1861–1947.* New Delhi: Concept Publishing, 1979.

GWYNN, MAJOR-GENERAL SIR CHARLES W. *Imperial Policing.* London: Macmillan, 1934.

HIBBERT, CHRISTOPHER. *King Mob. The Story of Lord George Gordon and the Riots of 1780.* London: Longmans, Green, 1958.

HOMES DUDDEN, F. *Henry Fielding. His Life, Works and Times.* Two vol. Oxford: Clarendon Press, 1952.

HOWGRAVE-GRAHAM, H.M. *Light and Shade at Scotland Yard.* London: John Murray, 1947.

HOWSON, GERALD. *Thief-Taker General. The Rise and Fall of Jonathan Wild.* London: Hutchinson, 1970.

IATROS (YATES, DAVID GRANT, DR): *A Biographical Sketch of the Life and Writings of Patrick Colquhoun Esq., LL.D.* London, 1818.

INGLETON, ROY D. *Police of the World.* New York: Charles Scribner's Sons, 1979.

International Security Directory, 1982–83. See Parker, C.G.A.

IRVINE, HAMISH. *The Diced Cap: The Story of Aberdeen City Police.* Aberdeen: The Chief Constable and Corporation of the city of Glasgow, 1972.

JACKSON, R.M. *The Machinery of Justice in England.* 6th ed. Cambridge: The University Press, 1972.

JEFFRIES, SIR CHARLES. *The Colonial Police.* London: Max Parrish, 1952.

JEYES, S.H., AND F.D. HOW. *The Life of Sir Howard Vincent.* London: George Allen, 1912.

JUDGE, ANTHONY. *The First Fifty Years: The Story of the Police Federation.* London: The Police Federation, 1968.

——, AND GERALD REYNOLDS. *The Night the Police Went on Strike.* London: Weidenfeld and Nicolson, 1968.

KELLY, WILLIAM AND NORA KELLY. *Policing in Canada.* Toronto: Macmillan, 1976.

LAURIE, PETER. *Scotland Yard: A Personal Inquiry.* London: George Allen and Unwin, 1978.

LESLIE-MELVILLE, R. *The Life and Work of Sir John Fielding.* London: Lincoln Williams, 1935.

LIECK, ALBERT. *Justice and Police in England.* London: Butterworths, 1929.

McCULLOUGH, H.M. "The Royal Ulster Constabulary." In *Police Studies,* vol. 4 (Winter 1982).

MARLOWE, JOYCE. *The Peterloo Massacre.* London: Rapp and Whiting, 1969.

MARSHALL, GEOFFREY. *Police and Government: The Status and Accountability of the English Constable.* London: Methuen, 1965.

MELVILLE LEE, W.L. *A History of Police in England.* (1901). Reprint ed. Montclair, NJ: Patterson Smith, 1971.

MILLER, WILBUR. *Cops and Bobbies: Police Authority in New York and London 1830–1870.* Chicago and London: University of Chicago Press, 1977.

MOSSE, GEORGE L. (Ed.). *Police Forces in History.* London, Beverly Hills: Sage, 1975.

MOYLAN, J.F. *Scotland Yard and the Metropolitan Police.* London and New York: G.P. Putnam's Sons, 1929.

O'BRIEN, G. *The Australian Police Forces.* Melbourne: Oxford University Press, 1960.

PARKER, C.G.A. *International Security Directory 1982–83.* Henley-on-Thames: Court and Judicial Publishing, 1982.

PARKER, K.A.L. "Hendon and After." In *Police Journal* (July 1980).

———. "The Constitutional Structure of the Metropolitan Police." In *Police Journal* (October 1980, and January 1981).

———: "The Educational Background of the Police." In *Police Journal* (October 1982).

Police: Monthly Magazine of the Police Federation of England and Wales. 1966–.

Police and Constabulary Almanac. Annually, since 1861. Henley-on-Thames: R. Hazell, 1983.

Police Journal. Quarterly. Chichester: Barry Rose, 1928–.

Police Review. Weekly. London: 1892–.

Police Studies. Quarterly. Cincinnati, OH: Anderson; Henley-on-Thames: Court and Judicial Publishing, 1978–.

POWIS, DAVID. *The Signs of Crime: A Field Manual for Police.* London: McGraw-Hill, 1977.

PRINGLE, PATRICK. *Hue and Cry: The Birth of the British Police.* London: Museum Press, 1955.

———. *The Thief-Takers.* London: Museum Press, 1958.

————. Ed. *Memoirs of a Bow Street Runner (Henry Goddard)*. London: Museum Press, 1956.

PROCTER, MAURICE. *No Proud Chivalry*. London: Longmans Green, 1947.

PULLING, CHRISTOPHER. *Mr. Punch and the Police*. London: Butterworths, 1964.

RADZINOWICZ, SIR LEON. *A History of English Criminal Law*. London: Stevens, 1948–68.

REITH, CHARLES. *The Police Idea: Its History and Evolution in England in the Eighteenth Century and After*. London: Oxford University Press, 1938.

————. *The Blind Eye of History*. A study of the origins of the present police era. (1952). Reprint ed. Montclair, NJ: Patterson Smith, 1975.

————. *A New Study of Police History*. Edinburgh: Oliver and Boyd, 1956.

REPPETTO, THOMAS A. *The Blue Parade*. New York: The Free Press; London: Collier Macmillan, 1978.

RIPLEY, HOWARD. *Police Forces of Great Britain and Ireland—their Amalgamations and their Buttons*. Henley-on-Thames, 1983.

ROLPH, C.H. (Ed.). *The Police and the Public*. London: Heinemann, 1962.

————: *Living Twice: An Autobiography*. London: Gollancz, 1974.

ROYAL COMMISSION ON THE POLICE, 1960. *Interim Report*. London: HMSO, 1960.

————. *Final Report*. London: HMSO, 1962.

RUMBELOW, DONALD. *I Spy Blue: The Police and Crime in the City of London from Elizabeth I to Victoria*. London: Macmillan, 1977.

SCARMAN, LORD. *The Scarman Report: The Brixton Disorders, 10–12 April 1981*. Harmondsworth: Penguin, 1982.

SELLWOOD, A.V. *Police Strike: 1919*. London: W.H. Allen, 1978.

SIMPSON, KEITH. *Forty Years of Murder: An Autobiography*. London: Harrap, 1978.

SLOAN, KENNETH. Public Order and the Police. London: Police Review, 1977.

ST. JOHNSTON, SIR ERIC. *One Policeman's Story*. London and Chichester: Barry Rose, 1978.

STANLEY, C.R. *The Purpose of a Lifetime: A Profile of Barbara Mary Denis de Vitré, O.B.E., 1905–1960*. Chichester: Barry Rose, 1972.

STEAD, PHILIP JOHN (Ed.). *Pioneers in Policing*. Montclair: Patterson Smith, 1977.

————. *The Police of France*. New York: Macmillan, 1983. London: Collier Macmillan, 1983.

TAMUNO, T.N. *The Police in Modern Nigeria*. Abadan: Abadan University Press, 1970.

THURSTON, GAVIN. *The Clerkenwell Riot. The Killing of Constable Culley*. London: George Allen and Unwin, 1967.

TOBIAS, J.J. *Crime and Industrial Society in the Nineteenth Century*. London: Batsford, 1967.

————. *Crime and Police in England: 1700–1900*. Dublin: Gill and Macmillan, 1979.

WADE, JOHN. *A Treatise on the Police and Crimes of the Metropolis*. (1829). Reprint ed. Montclair, NJ: Patterson Smith, 1972.

WATT, IAN A. *A History of the Hampshire and Isle of Wight Constabulary. 1839–1966*. Winchester: Hampshire and Isle of Wight Constabulary, 1967.

WEGG-PROSSER, CHARLES. *The Police and the Law*. London: Oyez, 1973.

WELLS, ROGER. *Insurrection: The British Experience 1795–1803*. Gloucester: Alan Sutton, 1983.

WENSLEY, FREDERICK PORTER. *Detective Days. The Record of Forty-two Years' Service in the Criminal Investigation Department*. London: Cassell, 1931.

WILLIAMS, CHRISTOPHER. *Prosecuting Officer*. London: Sweet and Maxwell, 1960.

YATES, DR DAVID GRANT. See Iatros.

Index